the **bikini** book

Kelly Killoren Bensimon

with 286 illustrations, 175 in colour

Thames & Hudson

CONTENTS

FOREWORD

I first designed a bikini in 1987. At the time, I was the designer for Hermès ready-to-wear, and the bikini was a part of my first summer collection for the house. In truth, I didn't give it much thought. How hard could it be to design a bikini? Very hard, it turns out. And for me, very interesting. I learned that I loved designing bikinis, enjoyed the challenges and constraints involved in creating such a specialized piece of clothing. I had more ideas than there were models on the runway. I launched my own swimwear line a few years later and have kept at it ever since. To me, a bikini is a bold collaboration between a designer and a woman. When it works, it's exhilarating. When it doesn't, it's an instant and obvious failure. The small size of the garment is as challenging to the designer as it is to the wearer (though I fully realize that she is the one stepping out into the sunlight wearing less than a meter of fabric). So for both of us, there's no margin for error and very little space in which to play. Then there is the issue of function, which is really up to the designer. A bikini has to stay up, it has to stay in place, and it must work for both swimming and tanning. To which I add my own conditions: I think a bikini should look natural. It must be comfortable. It has to be lightweight. Also, when you take it off, it shouldn't leave ugly red seam marks on your body. Bikini design never gets boring; in part that's because the fabrics keep evolving. The bikinis that my mother and her friends wore in the '60s were made of woven fabrics with elasticized borders and hooks for closures. Then came LYCRA® in the '70s, and bathing suits got softer, fit better, usually made with knit jersey.

By the '80s—when I started designing—the bikini had become rigid. It was the era of high-rise bottoms and tops made with foam cups. I hate that hard look. I think a bikini should be soft, with the support coming from the fabric and the construction. Really, a bikini's shape comes from a woman's body. Right now I'm working with wovens again, this time with double-elasticized yarns. Because there are technical aspects to successful bikini design, the emergence of new materials inevitably offers new possibilities.

Of course, some things don't change. Proportion is always crucial. Lines, too—you want the lines to run in the right places, to be the right width for the suit and the body. Seams have to work technically and aesthetically, and must be placed to enhance the shape of the body and the appeal of the design. I always design small bottoms—they're much more flattering. And I think color is less about trends than about a woman's skin color and the sun. I love neutral colors—cement, stone, flesh tones, and black. I think a dark brown bikini is the epitome of chic, while a white bikini is the hardest to wear (though dazzling when it works). In conclusion, the styling and color of a bikini may work in one setting, but be a wash in another. A stone-colored bikini that looks beautiful in Amagansett is too pale for the Caribbean, where a pastel pink might be just right. Only the woman wearing the suit can decide those things, which is part of the collaboration between the designer and the wearer. She trusts me to create a bikini that works, and I hope she is comfortable enough with my design to wear it with confidence. Because a bikini doesn't look like anything on a hanger.

INTRODUCTION

I will never forget the first time I saw a bikini. My parents had taken my grandparents on a vacation to Hawaii and returned bearing gifts. Mine and my sister's were bikinis. I grabbed one immediately, whipped off my clothes right there in the dining room, and put it on. I was 3. My older sister and my twin brother opened their presents as well, and soon we all stood proudly in our dining room sporting our new floral Hawaiian print cotton swimwear. Then my brother looked at his chest, and looked at my sister and me. He wasn't happy. We were wearing little cotton triangle tops. He, of course, wasn't. "Where's my top?" he protested at the top of his voice to my parents. I thought about lending him mine, but decided against it. Thirty years and two daughters later, I am still wearing bikinis. Admittedly, not the micro-mini floral styles I started with, but the ones I now prefer are not known for their coverage, either. My personal favorites range from low-slung to string, preferably made by the French company ERES or by German designer Tomas Maier.

I have always felt comfortable in a bathing suit or a bikini—more so than in any other article of clothing. To start with, wearing them was a huge part of my youth. Growing up, I was a competitive swimmer and wore a bathing suit every day for two hours plus. It is suggested that the bikini functions as a way of exposing the body and enticing sexual thoughts by hiding the erogenous zones—areas deemed too intimate to show. For me, however, the bikini is a vehicle for PTR (prime tanning rays). Which, coincidentally, is what inspired French mechanical engineer Louis Reard to invent the bikini in the first place.

The "scandalous" four triangles, which used only thirty inches of fabric, were named after Bikini Atoll in the Pacific Ocean, where on July 1, 1946, the U.S. Army was performing a series of nuclear bomb tests. The inception of the bikini, or "modern" bathing suit, came just four days later, on the fifth of July. It was as explosive as the atomic bomb itself. During that summer, Reard had spent days gazing at women lying on the beaches in St. Tropez. He'd noticed them rolling up and pulling down the tops and bottoms of their two-piece suits as far as possible to expose as much of their bodies to the sun as they could. Just over a year after World War II, the beaches were a safe haven again and became playgrounds once more. Men and women alike were craving the simple pleasures of summer's sea and sun. Reard was at the right place at the right time.

However, during the late '40s the revolutionary bikini was hardly worn—not by any respectable woman, anyway. Reard could not even find a model to premiere the suit at the well-known pool Piscine Molitor's fashion show. They all refused. Instead, the task fell to Casino de Paris nude dancer Micheline Bernardini. The impact was immediate. The bikini and the navel, the zone of contention, were put on the world's stage. One year later, in 1947, fashion photographer Toni Frissell photographed the suit. But America did not care: any woman caught wearing the bikini on American beaches was escorted off. In 1964, the Vatican even banned its usage in Catholic countries.

From its inception in 1946, it took the mainstream more than fifteen years to embrace—and wear—the bikini. In 1959, American bathing suit company Cole of California designed and mass-produced bikinis with bandeau tops and adjustable side ties. They were smaller and exposed more than the original deux-pièces. This fit perfectly with the sexual liberation of the '60s, which went hand-in-hand with the advent of the birth control pill. Surf, song, and the jet plane also helped export the bikini from the beaches of St. Tropez onto every teen in America. In 1960, Brian Hyland's "Itsy Bitsy Teenie Weenie Yellow Polka Dot Bikini" song was on the tip of everyone's tongue. In 1962, Ursula Andress came out of the water in a white bikini as Honey Ryder in *Dr. No*, and mousekeeter Annette Funicello wore a bikini in

Beach Party. Then in 1964, *Sports Illustrated* revealed Babette March on the cover in a modest bikini. From that moment, the bikini was legitimized and the phenomenon of the bikini model began. Women all over the world have wanted, and still want, to look like the bikini pioneer Bridgitte Bardot and ultimate sex symbol Raquel Welch. In the new revealing modern bathing suits, which incidentally resembled the original two-piece (the difference between the two bathing suits is the exposure of the navel), the emphasis was on a woman's curves; and her skin, her torso, and her breasts. In 1964, fashion designer Rudi Gernreich, with the help of a new synthetic fiber called LYCRA® took the idea of exposure a step further and created the monokini (3,000 suits were sold in one season), which led to topless sunbathing. Three years later, Bardot wore her string bikini as low as possible and took off her top at the Byblos Hotel in St. Tropez. Though she and Gernreich explored exhibitionism, the rest of the world did not follow in their footsteps.

What this exhibitionism did do, however, was telegraph the personal exploration synonymous with the '70s. By then, women had become less conscious of their bodies, and wore their bikinis in all shapes and sizes. Crochet, vinyl, lace, and leather bikinis, as well as adornments such as coins, fake fur, and beads, were emblematic of the liberated times. The erogenous zones exposed in the '60s were the breasts and the midriff. But, with the lower string-bikini bottoms of the '70s, attention shifted to the upper thighs. In Brazil, the thong-style "tanga" or the "sunga," the men's version of the bikini—inspired by sumo wrestlers— became popular, especially in Rio de Janerio. This new bikini, which exposed more than just the upper thighs, then traveled from the beaches of Ipanema and Rio to the gyms of America. The "tanga," "thong," or "dental floss" did one thing: cover the groin area. This was perfect for the newly aerobicized bodies of the '80s. Well-defined buttocks were enhanced with the tanga. The high-cut leg made all legs look longer and more shapely, and LYCRA® kept everything in place. The tanga also inspired a new breed of bikinis in America: the roll-down. With this, you could expose as much of your body as you saw fit; it was a personalized bikini.

In the '80s, women—and men—were more than just fit; they were athletic. Fabrics like neoprene (traditionally used for wet suits) facilitated the fit of the new athletic bikini. Amazonian women's volleyball player Gabrielle Reece put the sports bikini (similar to a jogging bra) on the map. I will never forget the day she asked me to come visit her at the beach in California. I asked if I could help her while she was practicing—my only other option would have been to sit and sunbathe and look incredibly lazy. Gabby told me the only way I could help was to retreive the balls that went out of the court. I was wearing my favorite ultra-skimpy ERES string bikini. All her teammates had on sports bikini tops and briefs. I ran in the sand like crazy trying to get their balls. I am not sure which part was worse: trying to keep my string bikini up, or pretending that I wasn't extremely exhausted. I quickly realized why they wore athletic bra top bikinis. Function over form had something to do with it…

In the twenty-first century, the bikini is here to stay. From the pinups who popularized the *deux–pièces* to the *Sports Illustrated* swimsuit models who have replaced Farrah Fawcett on every boy's wall to Princess Diana in the Caribbean surf, the bikini is the ultimate vehicle. Whether it is tanned skin you want to show, curves you want to hide, defined abdominal muscles you want to expose, or hips you want to enhance, the bikini has evolved with the times and the fads, even with the popularization of piercing and tattoos. What was a rite of passage has even evolved with the ideology that 40 is the new 20. The bikini is the Peter Pan of swimwear. Every woman of every age is wearing a bikini. It has transcended scandals and boycotts and will always remain the most sensual article of clothing next to lingerie. *Le bikini* could only have been invented by a man.

bi•ki•ni, *noun.*
[F, fr. *Bikini*, atoll of
the Marshall Islands]
(1947). **1. a.** a very brief
close-fitting two-piece
bathing suit worn by
women. **b.** an abbreviated
two-piece bathing suit
2. a man's or woman's
low-cut brief.

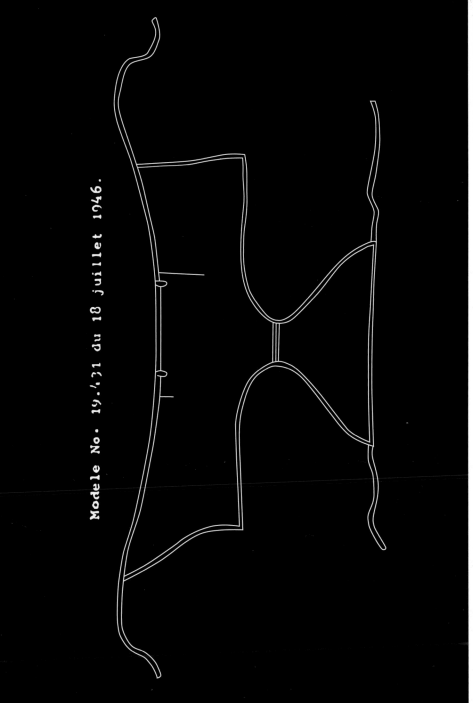

Modele No. 19.431 du 18 juillet 1946.

CHAPTER 1

HISTORY

THE FIRST BIKINI

In 1946, one year after the end of World War II, two French designers become famous for creating the bikini swimsuit: Jacques Heim and Louis Reard. Heim is credited with creating "the world's smallest bathing suit," also known as the "atome" (a play on the smallest known particle), which he introduced as a sexier alternative to the two-piece suit favored by Hollywood sirens such as Dorothy Lamour. It is said that Heim hired skywriters to promote "the world's smallest bathing suit." Reard, a French automotive engineer and son of a lingerie shop owner, also tried his hand at designing the ultimate in swimwear. Unlike its contemporary, the *deux-pièces* or two-piece, which was traditionally a halter-style top with a broad bottom covering the navel and hips, Reard's bikini would expose more skin than ever. Inspired by sunbathers on the beaches of St. Tropez whom he observed rolling down their two-piece swimsuits to expose more skin for tanning, Reard believed the moment was right to introduce a more liberating and, as he saw it, more practical option. Days later, this pioneer sent skywriters with the message: "Bikini, smaller than the smallest bathing suit in the world." The sensation hit as hard as the epochal event of the atomic bomb tests on July 1, 1946, which were being conducted by the U.S. Army on the Bikini Atoll lagoon in the Marshall Islands in the Pacific Ocean. "They call them bikinis for they don't cover them atoll," one journalist quipped.

A fourth-century Roman mosaic (opposite) depicting an athletic scene with female gymnasts in two-piece suits.

Micheline Bernardini in the first bikini designed by Reard, 1946

EVOLUTION OF THE BIKINI

While it was surrounded with scandal, the bikini was hardly the first garment to show so much skin. Dating back to 1400 BC, two-piece garments were depicted in wall paintings, and Greek women wore bikini-like garments for athletic purposes. The traditional dress of women in sultans' harems resembles modern swimwear, and in the 1920s, burlesque dancers wore this silhouette in their acts, as did Paris showgirls and vaudeville performers. The Hays Code of 1930 and the rise of censorship in American films during the early '30s enforced certain behavior and dress codes for the big screen. This set a standard of appropriate ethics for women all over the world. But though the Hays Code did not ban the two-piece, it did ban exposure of the navel.

In 1932, French designer Madeleine Vionnet exposed the bare midriff in an evening dress, which forecasted the acceptability of more skin exposure. Finally, in 1935 the American designer Claire McCardell designed the cutout maillot—a forerunner of the bikini. The bandeau top, cutout side panels, and hip-hugging bottom concealed the navel, a zone of contention.

The *deux-piéces* or two-piece (a halter top and full, high-waisted bottom), became the fashion for pinups and movie stars like Esther Williams, and subsequently the everywoman who followed fashion. If it was good enough for pinups, then it was good enough for the American woman.

Chili Williams, "the Polka-Dot Girl," glamorized the two-piece swimming costume. Discovered by a modeling agent in Fire Island, Williams became famous for her portraits (opposite).

THE STRING
AND NUDE STYLES WILL
FAIL OF THEMSELVES.

LOUIS REARD

At a fashion show at the well-known Piscine Molitor, a swimming pool in Paris, on July 5, 1946, Reard presented *le bikini.* No respectable model would agree to wear the navel- and buttocks-exposing suit in the show with the exception of Micheline Bernardini, a strip-dancer from the Casino de Paris.

What is evident is that both Heim and Reard were inspired by detailed newspaper reports about atomic testing taking place at the time on the Bikini Atoll in the South Pacific four days prior. During the period following World War II, when military power was laudable and very much a part of social consciousness, terms like "blonde bombshell" and "atomic"—an adjective used to describe just about anything of intensity—were on everyone's lips. Simultaneously making light of his design and poking fun at the media, Reard not only named his suit after the island where nuclear testing was taking place, he constructed it from a fabric of printed newspaper clippings.

PINUPS

AN AMERICAN DREAM

The 1950s dawned with a new style of pinup. During the early '50s and the McCarthy era, Communism and the fear of the Cold War was on everyone's mind. The conservative nuclear family in America had a two-bedroom home and a car, but also lived in fear of an atomic bomb exploding. The ultra-feminine and modest pinups of the time reflected these conservative attitudes. They traditionally wore the two-piece top that supported a fuller figure. These tops were enhanced and rigidly constructed with a zipper and bra-like "foundations," as Marilyn Monroe called them, and which

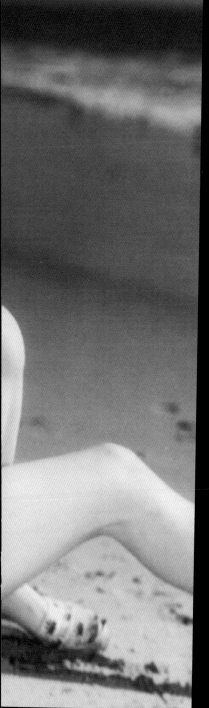

Jayne Mansfield swore by. Esther William[s] the most well-known swimwear pinup of th[e] decade, was against the scandalous bikin[i]. "Young girls," Williams said, "can wear [a] couple of Dixie cups and a fishing line if the[y] want, but that's not my lady. A bathing suit [is] the least amount of clothing you are going t[o] wear in public, so you had better give it som[e] thought. A bikini is a thoughtless act."

Regardless of what Williams thought, swimsu[it] manufacturer Cole of California introduced i[ts] first mass-produced bikini at the end of th[e] '50s, a concoction that included a slightl[y] stiff constructed bra that balanced tensio[n] between a bandeau and halter ties. *Vogu[e]* magazine said, "[the bikini] is rightful as th[e] sexiest suit on the beach."

Less conservative and more established international stars who were equally prepared to make navel displays followed. This lon[g] list included the likes of Monroe, who ha[d] modeled bikinis continuously since the lat[e] 1940s but whose stature as a star/icon an[d] forays into nudity eclipsed her reputation a[s] a bikini girl.

Previous pages: Rita Hayworth,1947 (left). Esther Williams (right). Left: Marilyn Monroe, c. 1940.

BUNNY YEAGER

PIONEER PHOTOGRAPHER, MODEL, AND DESIGNER

In 1954, model, photographer, and bikini designer Bunny Yeager started to photograph women in bikinis that she made out of cotton and held together with rope or even daisies. The bikinis made by Yeager were incredibly innovative and scandalous for the time. Yeager became an overnight success due to her provocative photographs

Magazines for men such as *Playboy* could not get enough of her images.

The photos typically portrayed girl-next-door types posing in some of the sexiest, most provocative bathing suits of the time. By the '60s, Yeager's pinups foreshadowed even bigger things to come. Her girl-next-door pinup was on every man's mind.

THE MIAMI HURRICANE

VOL. XXIII   UNIVERSITY OF MIAMI, CORAL GABLES, FLA., SEPTEMBER 2 1949   No

WHAT NOT TO WEAR at the North pole is demonstrated quite well by University student Bunny Yeager. One of the most widely photographed girls in the country, Bunny started her modeling career two years ago when she won the title of Florida Trailercoach Queen. She was picked from a field of over 40 contestants at the Sportsman's and Trailercoach Show in Miami. Since that time, Bunny has won several other beauty contests, and has appeared on the covers of many publications. The 19-year-old coed hopes to continue her modeling career, and from the way she wears those two bandanas, it doesn't look like she'll have much trouble.

My first "real" bikini suit.

JAYNE MANSFIELD

THE FEMALE JUNGLE

The ultimate '50s pinup and rival to movie star Marilyn Monroe, Jayne Mansfield loved her status as a sex symbol. "I like being a pinup," she said. "There is nothing wrong with it." With a forty-one-inch chest, Mansfield was considered too sexy for the big screen and never became the star she wanted to be. But *Playboy* magazine made her Playmate of the Month in February 1955—her glamorous sex-symbol image wasn't too much for them. In a 1957 *Life* magazine shoot, a buoyant Mansfield posed in a pool of bikinied water bottles. The woman loved pink and thought that "women should be pink and be cuddly for a man," lived in a pink house, and married the famous bodybuilder Mickey Hargitay. But it wasn't pink that made her a sensation—it was her first appearance in a red bikini, where the press headlined "Jayne points out Jane."

Opposite: The infamous red bikini.

Following pages: Mansfield and Mickey Hargitay (left), and the legendary *Life* magazine shoot (right).

Jayne Mansfield works
her forty-one-inch chest
in a variety of styles.

ANIMAL MAGNETISM

THE GIRL IN THE LEOPARD BIKINI

With the popularity of the Tarzan films of the '50s, leopard took off. By 1955, the feline mood was portrayed all over the silver screen. Models posed for the cameras in leopard-print swimsuits. Model and 1955's Miss Pinup Girl of the World Bettie Page—also known as "the naughty girl-next-door"—became a pop culture icon with her jet black hair, fearless bangs, and sex

Opposite: Carmen Miranda in Hollywood.
Above: Leopard in St. Tropez, 1977.

kitten look. (Even modest actresses such as Donna Reed wore the leopard-print two-piece.) Leopard was not only associated with provocative jungle adventures and pinups, but also with fur, and fur connotes luxury. If luxury was good enough for the pinups, it was good enough for the mainstream, even if it was just printed.

CHAPTER 2

BIKINI IN FILM

In 1956, *And God Created Woman* was released in France, mesmerizing audiences with sex and the sensuality of Brigitte Bardot, glowing in a gingham bikini—or in nothing at all.

Two years later, Roger Vadim's directorial debut, crossed the Atlantic, revolutionizing foreign film and seducing Americans with the bikini, fresh off the beaches of the French Riviera. During a period of regrowth after World War II, this film inaugurated the importance of the bikini.

After *And God Created Woman,* the bikini's presence in film spiraled. Next came the Swiss bombshell Ursula Andress emerging from the ocean in a white bikini in the 1962 James Bond film *Dr. No.*

In the early '60s, the bikini was catalyzed by the likes of Sandra Dee and Annette Funicello in the teen-surfer beach movie series. The first, entitled *Beach Party,* starred Annette Funicello, a former Mickey Mouse Club actress, emphatically not in a bikini, at the request of her mentor, Walt Disney, who insisted that she wear the more modest two-piece. After six sequels to *Beach Party,* Disney finally agreed to allow Funicello to appear on-screen in

Opposite: Actress Lauren Hutton makes a splash in *Paper Lion,* 1968.

47

the modern bikini, and in *How to Stuff a Wild Bikini* (1965), she finally exposes her navel. If Annette can wear one, then all of the fashion-conscious teenagers could wear one too. This film initiated a whole new genre of movies: the California beach movie, featuring nice girls, big cars, surf, sun, and Beach Boys music. The baby boomers were now teens and ready to explore the world around them in the latest fashion attire: the barely there bikini.

But these initial silhouettes were modest exposures of the California surf crowd. The "Itsy Bitsy Teenie Weenie Yellow Polka Dot Bikini" generated another buying spree of bikinis. Featured in the 1962 comedy film *One, Two, Three*, Brian Hyland's catchy song was played during the interrogation of a spy. The lyrics talk about a woman who "is afraid to come out of the water" because she is too embarrassed by her attire: the yellow polka-dot bikini.

It wasn't until the '60s that the bikini entered mainstream culture. Annette Funicello, star of the *Bikini Beach* series, wore a two-piece in all but the last film, *How To Stuff a Wild Bikini*.

In Vincent Price's spy spoof *Dr. Goldfoot and the Bikini Machine* (1965), a demented doctor invents an army of bikini-clad robots in a scheme to control the world's richest men. But one of the most unforgettable bikini images that comes to mind for many people isn't really a bikini at all. Actress Raquel Welch appeared in an animal-hide bikini as a cavewoman in the 1966 movie *One Million Years B.C.* From Bardot to Welch, Ludivine Sagnier to Ursula Andress, the bikini has made movie stars out of actresses.

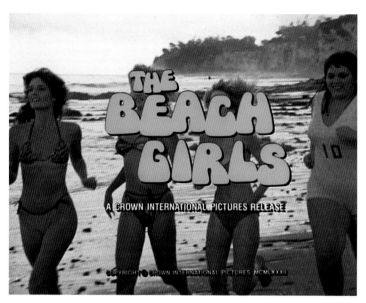

Opposite (clockwise from top): Dyan Cannon and Natalie Wood in *Bob & Carol & Ted & Alice* (1969); a team of fembots in *Dr. Goldfoot and the Bikini Machine* (1965); **Joan and Jackie Collins on a film set.**

This page: **A poster for** *The Beach Girls* (1982) **(top), and Frankie Avalon** in *Beach Blanket Bingo* (1965) **(bottom).**

**INNERS
ERTS...**

g course in

**BIRDS
BEES
BIKINIS**

*in six very
sy lessons*

STARRING

**ANNETTE FUNICELLO
DWAYNE HICKMAN**
BRIAN DONLEVY
BUSTER KEATON
BEVERLY ADAMS
HARVEY LEMBECK
JOHN ASHLEY · JODY McCREA
AND GUEST STAR
MICKEY ROONEY

**Thrills and spills
in the wildest
MOTORCYCLE RACE
ever run!**

61

AMERICAN INTERNATIONAL PRESENTS
"PAJAMA PARTY" Ⓤ
starring TOMMY KIRK · ANNETTE FUNICELLO
ELSA LANCHESTER · HARVEY LEMBECK · JESSE WHITE
JODY McCREA · BEN LESSY · DONNA LOREN · SUSAN HART
BOBBI SHAW · CANDY JOHNSON
WITH SPECIAL GUEST STARS BUSTER KEATON and DOROTHY LAMOUR
IN PATHECOLOR and PANAVISION (R)
FROM ANGLO AMALGAMATED FOR WARNER-PATHE RELEASE

IT TAKES A CONFIDENT WOMAN TO WEAR A BIKINI WELL— AND CONFIDENCE IS SEXY.... NO MATTER WHAT YOUR SIZE.

JENNA LYONS

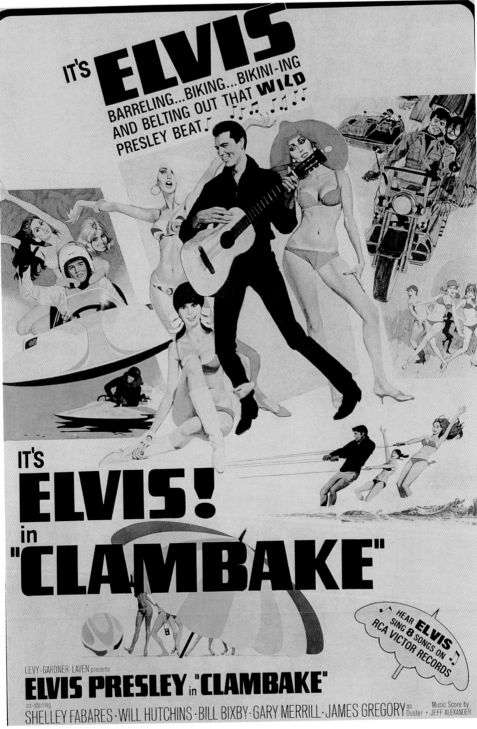

WHAT IS SEXY?

LUDIVINE SAGNIER IN 'SWIMMING POOL'

ELLEN BARKIN

RAQUEL WELCH

In 1963, journalist Gloria Steinem wrote her first book, *The Beach Book,* which featured a sun reflector on the inside cover and detailed the art of sun worshipping. Raquel Welch's dark skin and curvaceous figure is emblematic of the '60s: sexy and tan. In 1966, Welch became the ultimate sex symbol and a pop culture icon in her mammoth fur bikini in the film *One Million Years B.C.* But it was in the '70s that Raquel—now world famous for her barely there bikinis and minidresses—took off. Women were less self-conscious of their bodies—and that mood showed in the latest bikini designs. Bikinis in such fabrics as crochet, lace, and vinyl, with adornments like coins, fake fur, and beads were all the rage during the liberated '70s. And tan was in.

37-22-35: Raquel Welch's success started with the bikini and, of course her measurements. After appearing in *Life* magazine, Hollywood couldn't get enough of this "glamazon."

In the '60s, Welch takes in the sun (above). And Welch on the film sets of *The Last of Sheila* (1973), **(left) and** *The Biggest Bundle of Them All* (1968), **(right).**

THE BOND GIRL

ARMED, DANGEROUS, AND WEARING A BIKINI

In 1962, in the first James Bond film, actress Ursula Andress emerged from the sea in a white bikini. From that scene alone, men and women alike had a new empowered female sex symbol. Men fantasized about her, and women wanted to look like her. (The white suit, which was constructed from one of Andress's own bras, sold for $140,000 at a Christie's auction in London in 2001.) In 2002, actress Halle Berry in *Die Another Day* modernized Andress's *Dr. No* look. Swept up on the beach in a bright orange bikini, Berry's Bond Girl is every bit as charged. Adding fuel to the fire, these very sexy swimsuits were accessorized with white leather hipholsters that held hunting knives. The message: the Bond Girl is independent, resourceful, and especially dangerous. From Britt Ekland in *The Man in the Golden Gun* (1974) to Caroline Munroe in *The Spy Who Loved Me* (1977) to Kim Basinger in *Never Say Never Again* (1983), the Bond Girl in a bikini is quintessentially sexy. So much so that the bikini has become as central for a Bond Girl as a gun and a martini are for James.

Shirley Eaton, Honor Blackman and Tania Mallett in *Goldfinger*

Preceding pages:
Halle Berry in *Die Another Day* (left)
and Ursula Andress in *Dr. No* (right).

This page:
Ursula Andress (left), a movie poster
for *Dr. No* (below), and Andress
and Sean Connery on the film set
(opposite).

THIS BIKINI MADE ME A SUCCESS.

LOO7 UP!

This page (clockwise from left):
Ursula Andress in *Dr. No*; Martine Beswicke in *Thunderball* (1965); Jill St John in *Diamonds are Forever* (1971); Joanna Pettet in *Casino Royale* (1967).

Opposite: Movie poster for *You Only Live Twice* (1967).

Preceding pages (clockwise):
Movie poster for *Dr. No*, Britt Ekland, Mie Hama in *You Only Live Twice* (left). Maud Adams, Roger Moore, and Britt Ekland in *The Man with the Golden Gun* (right).

SEAN CONNERY IS JAMES BOND

IN IAN FLEMING'S

"YOU ONLY LIVE TWICE"

...and "TWICE" is the only way to live!

Presented by **ALBERT R. BROCCOLI** and **HARRY SALTZMAN** · Directed by **LEWIS GILBERT** · Screenplay by **ROALD DAHL**

Produced by **ALBERT R. BROCCOLI** and **HARRY SALTZMAN** · Music by **JOHN BARRY** · Production designed by **KEN ADAM** · **PANAVISION**®

TECHNICOLOR® Released thru **UNITED ARTISTS**

CHAPTER 3

FRENCH RIVIERA

If there's one spot in the world where bikini history has been made, it's the French Riviera. And if there's one person who popularized both the bikini and the region, it's Brigitte Bardot. In the early '50s, she brought the bikini to the beaches of St. Tropez when she starred in Roger Vadim's film *And God Created Woman* (1956). Only ten years after World War II, Bardot conquered hearts around the world by soaking up rays in her Vichy suit. In her teeny bikini, Bardot was the image of a simple young woman, poles apart from Christian Dior's New Look, so popular at the time.

Naturally provocative and constantly eyed by the media, Bardot took it a step further when she sunbathed on the terrace of St. Tropez's Hotel Byblos. She was quickly imitated by thousands of other beach bums, who made going topless the new symbol of a woman's freedom. The beaches of St. Tropez—and especially the legendary Club 55, inextricably linked to the filming of *And God Created Woman*—were the first places to host the new fashion. And so began the myth of the small French port town and its free spirit. It was the start of the immigration of swingers captivated by tanning girls on vacation, each wearing only half a bikini.

Brigitte Bardot, the bikini, and St. Tropez became one during the actress's career.

91

This page (clockwise from left): Brigitte Bardot in *The Girl in the Bikini* (1952); in *The Night Heaven Fell* (1958); and the actresss posing in an impromptu bikini.

Opposite: Bardot in *The Night Heaven Fell*.

This page:
Alain Delon in St. Tropez
(left); Valérie Kaprisky (belo
in *The Year of the Jellyfish*.

Opposite page:
Actress Catherine Deneuve
with her fiancé, director
Roger Vadim, in 1962.

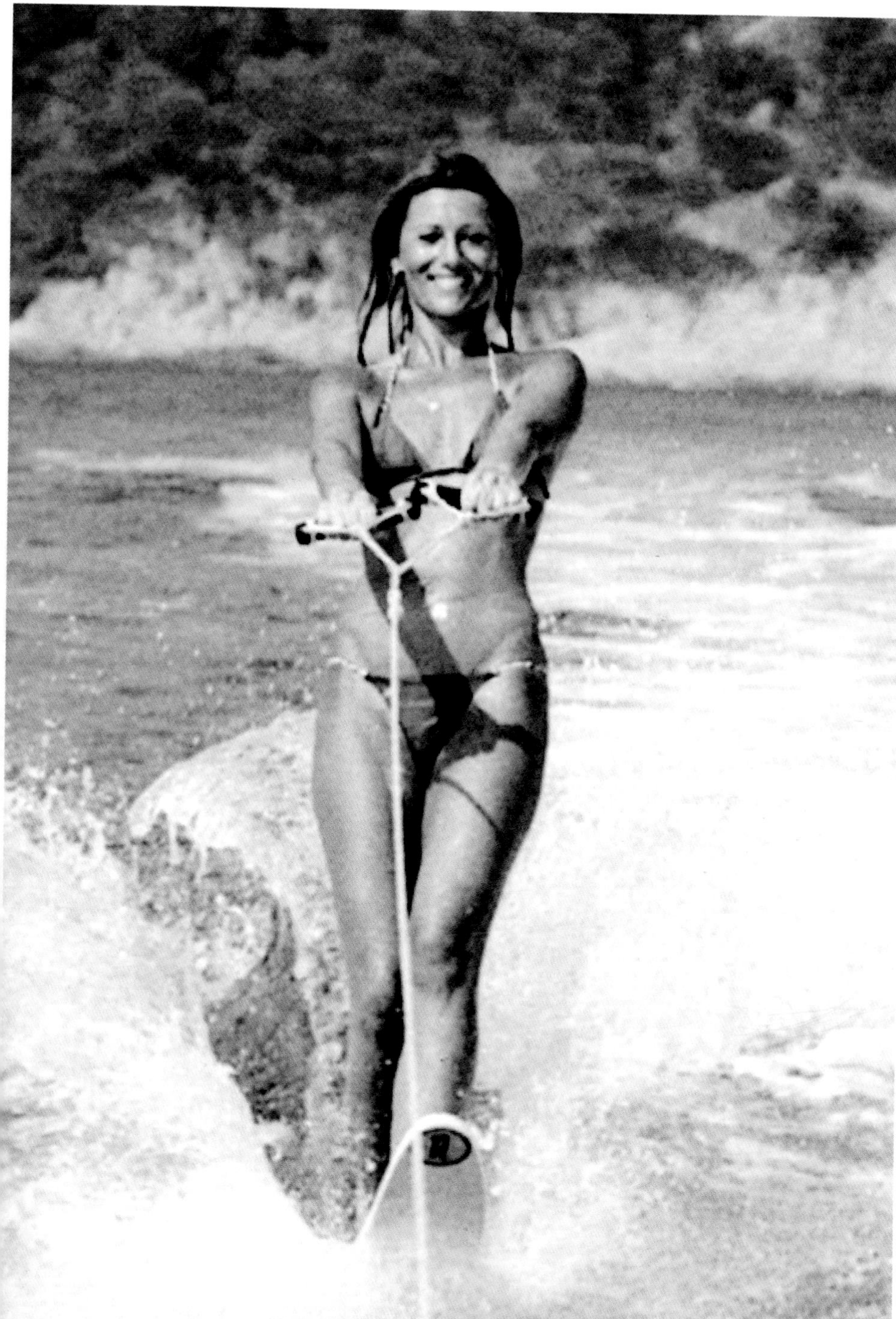

French singer Sheila on water skis

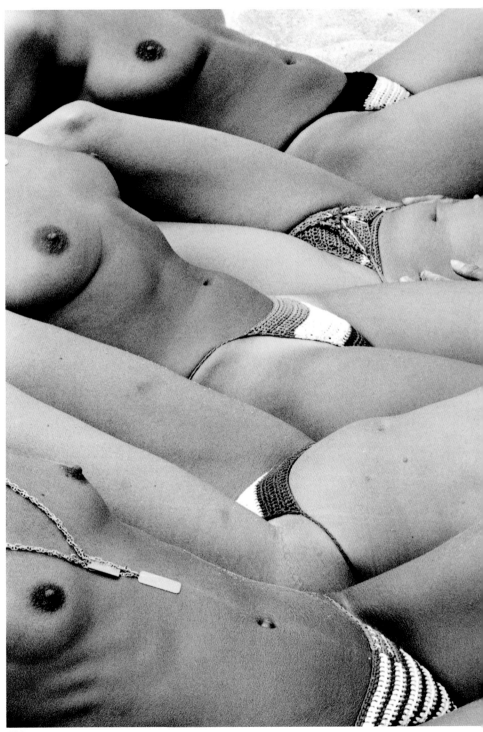

NO ROAD GOES
RIGHT THROUGH ST. TROPEZ.
THERE IS JUST ONE THAT
LEADS YOU TO THE VILLAGE,
BUT NO FURTHER. IF YOU WANT
TO LEAVE, YOU HAVE
TO GO BACK ON YOUR TRACKS.
BUT WILL YOU WANT
TO LEAVE?

COLETTE

CABINES.DOUCHES

WHAT HAPPENED NEXT
WAS LIKE A TRIGGER—THE START
OF A FREE-FOR-ALL. PLAYBOYS
FROM ALL OVER THE WORLD TURNED UP
TO WOO INTERNATIONAL STARS,
THE JET SET TREATED THE PLACE LIKE
ITS BASE CAMP, AND MILLIONAIRES
HAD PALACES BUILT ALL AROUND.
HELICOPTERS FILLED THE SKIES,
SWOOPING OVER SUPERLUXURY YACHTS
WHERE PRETTY PRINCESSES
SHED THEIR PREJUDICES.

BRIGITTE BARDOT

THE JET SET

In the years just after World War II, the emergence of the bikini symbolized the return of hedonism and an appetite for life's light side. Rome and Fellini's unforgettable *La Dolce Vita* lay the groundwork for this new culture, and the film, which was innovative in many ways, also exposed the workings of the paparazzi. By capturing celebrities in their most vulnerable moments, these star hunters would unconsciously help establish new trends. The images began to accumulate. Bikinis revealed athletic bodies, sensual bodies, teasing bodies, or good-girl bodies. From Jayne Mansfield to Sophia Loren, from Laura Antonelli to Jane Fonda, Monica Vitti to Kate Moss, ever since the '50s we all know the state of a celebrity's physique, thanks to the bikini. But the media doesn't stop at the movies. It has also showed us the pretty anatomies of Jacqueline Kennedy Onassis (remember the disrespect for her privacy on Skorpios Island), Princess Caroline and Princess Stephanie of Monaco (who once designed her own line of bathing suits) and Lady Di (who only wore Gottex and who spent her last summer enjoying the South of France).

BIKINI IS THE LAST EXQUISITE SHIELD BEFORE THE NAKED TRUTH.

DIANA PICASSO

Pablo Picasso receives a kiss from a bikini-clad girl in the stalls at a bullfight in 1956 (above), and the artist lounging on the beach (opposite).

Following pages:
Artist Salvador Dalí with Raquel Welch and his abstract portrait of her.

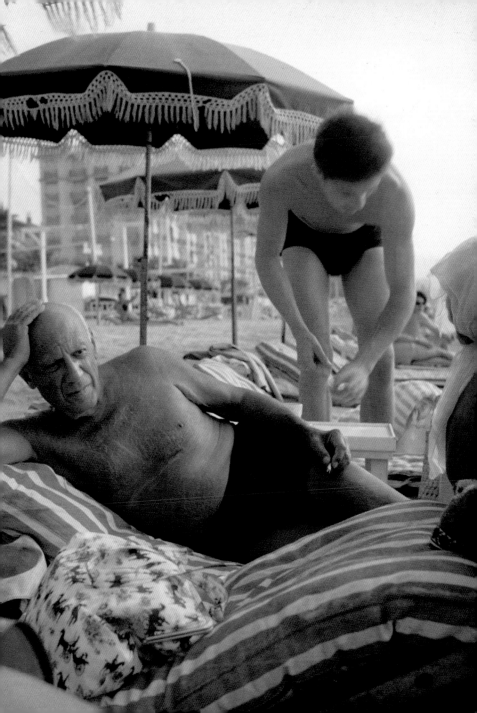

CHAPTER 4
THE BIKINI ISSUE

During the '70s, a new breed of model took the world by storm: the California girl. Cheryl Tiegs was its epitome: beautiful, shiny hair, tan, with perfect white teeth and a healthy look. As the ultimate all-American girl, Tiegs superseded the calender girl. She was approachable. Every woman wanted to be her, and every man wanted to be with her. Appearing on magazine covers from *Time* to *Vogue*, Tiegs also became a staple of the annual *Sports Illustrated* swimsuit issue. A three-time cover-model, Tiegs caused the biggest stir with an interior shot in 1978, when she wore a white fishnet bathing suit that exposed her nipples. It was said that more than 340 subscriptions were canceled in protest.

The '80s were the decade of excess. Everything was larger than life. Even in Europe, the idea of the ultimate was exploited with French designers like Thierry Mugler and Italian fashion designer Gianni Versace, who made their embellished designs and the models who wore them seem larger than life. The idea of the "super model," which transformed models into stars, exploded with the advent of music television, or MTV. French photographer Gilles Bensimon also had an idea. For the special beauty issue of the weekly French *Elle* magazine, Bensimon created and photographed the story "The Most Beautiful Girl in the World." Each model had an issue dedicated exclusively to her. She was photographed in a fashion story and a beauty story, and was interviewed. This was the advent of the supermodel. Every model wanted to become her. And every girl all over the world wanted to look like her.

A signed poster of the dirty blond and beautiful Tiegs, resplendent in a pink bikini, represents the epitome of sexy in the '70s.

Cheryl Tiegs

131

BEAUTY WHEN MOST UNCLOTHED IS CLOTHED BEST.

PHINEAS FLETCHER

Naomi Campbell in Dolce & Gabbana (left) and Christian Dior (right), 2002

IT IS AN EXCUSE TO WEAR LINGERIE IN PUBLIC. BECAUSE IT IS PRETTY MUCH A BRA AND PANTY, IF YOU THINK ABOUT IT, WITH A LITTLE BIT MORE LYCRA.

TYRA BANKS

Fernanda Tavares in a Josephine Loka silk printed bikini, 2000

SPORTS ILLUSTRATED

THE LEGEND OF THE SWIMSUIT ISSUE

As the Academy Awards is to the evening gown, the *Sports Illustrated* swimsuit issue is to the bikini. Whether made from green grass, chain mail, or body paint, each year, this much-hyped issue is traditionally stuffed with bikinis and the incredible bodies who wear them.

In Winter 1964, before the height of the sexual revolution in America, *Sports Illustrated* featured a bikini for the first time on its cover on model Babette March. And from that moment on, the bikini was legitimized. The decision to showcase a tanned and pretty model in a white bikini, rather than a sports star was made by none other than a Frenchman, Andre Laguerre. Laguerre, the legendary managing editor credited with bringing in top writers like George Plimpton and Dan Jenkins, and photographers Walter Ioos and Neil Lieger in the '60s and '70s, dreamed up the bikini-clad cover as an antedote to the slow period for sports during the winter months.

The first *Sports Illustrated* **cover to feature a bikini, opposite, was released, with controversy, in the winter of 1964.**

Sports Illustrated

KEARNS FIGHT MEN

JANUARY 20, 1964   25 CENTS

A
SKIN DIVER'S
GUIDE TO THE
CARIBBEAN

FUN IN THE SUN
ON COZUMEL

Cover model Petra Nemcova, 2003

Sports Illustrated

BODY PAINTING
RICK REILLY GETS NAKED
BEHIND-THE-SCENES PHOTOS

Too Much Fun

*Hottest Models,
Coolest Places
Around the World*

PETRA NEMCOVA *in Barbados*

A SWIMSUIT MYSTERY
by CARL HIAASEN

WINTER 2003 | DISPLAY UNTIL
www.si.com | 5/23/03

148

Turn over a
new leaf
Try vegetarian

GoVeg.com **PeTA**

152

THE BIKINI
IS ARGUABLY THE MOST
REVOLUTIONARY
ITEM OF CLOTHING SINCE
THE FIG LEAF.

DEREK LAM

MYTHOLOGY

PLAYBOY & PLAYMATES

SEX AND THE BIKINI

Midwestern-born journalist, Hugh Hefner took the idea of fantasy and fantasizing a step further. Hefner created a men's magazine called *Playboy* that has interesting articles to read and beautiful women to look at. The first issue of the magazine featured Marilyn Monore and sold over 50,000 copies. The marriage of evocative and provocative has made him the king of the most beautiful women in the world, and an arbiter of ultimate sex symbols. Pamela Anderson is a product of Hefner's amazing recipe: voluptuous, blonde, and beautiful. Though Anderson took her bikini off to pose for *Playboy*, she put on a white string-bikini to wed rocker Tommy Lee.

Playboy's "Covers" string-bikini, printed with vintage magazine covers, makes for another sexy marriage.

ENTERTAINMENT FOR MEN   JUNE 60 cents

PLAYBOY

A TOAST TO BIKINIS

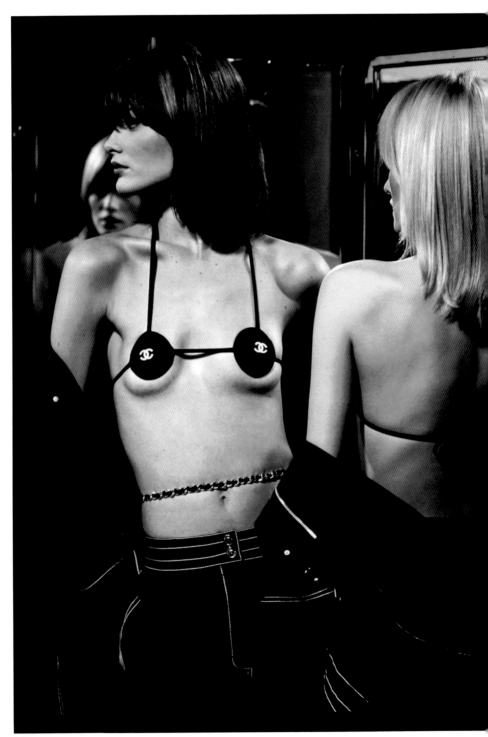

CHAPTER 5
FASHION

With the introduction of the bikini, the spectacle of the female body became the driving engine behind an expanding swimwear industry. For fashion designers, the bikini represented new terrain and a revolutionary vehicle for expression. The styles born out of the '50s were particularly innovative, due to a happy combination of willing Hollywood starlets and an established swimwear industry based in Los Angeles. Cole of California, Catalina, and Jantzen became top manufacturers, and many sportswear designers, including Tom Brigance, Claire McCardell, and Carolyn Schnurer, began to include swimwear in their collections. Schnurer in particular embraced the bikini, and fashion photographer Toni Frissell's 1947 provocative image of a strong, supple model stretched out poolside in one of her tiny designs remains an iconic image of an early bikini. By 1959, Cole of California presented its first mass-produced bikini in the U.S.

The eye-patch bikini by designer Karl Lagerfeld for Chanel.

FABRIC AND TEXTURE

The '50s also foreshadowed the major textile innovations that would shape the swimsuit in the decades to come. In the '30s, Lastex, an elastic yarn trademarked by U.S. Rubber, was blended with various other fibers to open up textural possibilities and glamour in swimwear. Lastex, in combination with cotton, wool, and rayon was dominant in swimwear in the 1950s. In 1939, DuPont invented nylon, which offered stretch and color retention not possible with Lastex, and in 1959, DuPont also developed LYCRA®, a synthetic fiber with inherent elasticity. Later that year, the legendary swimsuit manufacturer Gottex was one of the first to premiere the fiber in a collection of trendy prints.

According to contemporary designer Tracy Feith, with the advent of LYCRA®, swimsuits in general changed. "Suits became more high-tech," states Feith, "because the material lent itself to that. With LYCRA®, you can cut a square and make it as tight as you want."

Feith classifies the bikini into two sorts: the structured bikini, emblematic of the conservative '40s and '50s, and the '60s string-bikini, a sexier cousin of the original Reard suit. For his own designs, Feith prefers floral Hawaiian aloha patterns, paisleys, and traditional prints such as leopard, polka dots, gingham, Indian designs, and florals. These themes are reminiscent of another time, he explains, "like an old postcard."

A BIKINI REPRESENTS THE ULTIMATE IN BODY SCULPTING. IT CAN BE BOTH CONCEALING AND REVEALING. A SWIMSUIT ENHANCES THE NATURAL FEMALE FORM, ALLOWING FOR THE INDIVIDUAL WEARER'S BEAUTY TO EXPRESS ITSELF.

BRETTE SANDLER

Christina Kruse, 1995

SIXTIES AND SEVENTIES

By the late '60s, the modesty of the preceding decades was rendered obsolete. Boning, constructed bra cups, and linings were still used, but nylon and LYCRA® blends enabled relaxed forms. At the same time, the bikini brief, popular in underwear design, became the preferred bikini bottom, with a below-the-navel waistline and a slightly higher-cut leg. By 1965, Italian designer Emilio Pucci fashioned his signature geometric-printed silk jersey blend into bikinis, which *Vogue* celebrated by featuring a shocking pink version. The Pucci bikini had an underwire top with a back closure and halter strap, paired with a low-rise brief.

In the '60s, mod was all the rage. American designer Betsy Johnson was making plastic dresses, English designer Mary Quant created her famous prints, Andre Courrèges sent geometric minidresses down the runway, and the New York store Paraphernalia was on the mind of every teenager. Big, bold colors led the way on everything from bikinis to glasses. Demure was out, and exploration was in. For the bikini, that meant an explosion of playful design, including attached flowers, shiny PVC fabric, and cheeky zippers built in for easy access.

By the '70s, most linings and foundation components of the bikini were abandoned in favor of ease of movement. The 70s also marked the introduction of a perennial favorite swimsuit design—the string bikini. Defined by string closures at the sides

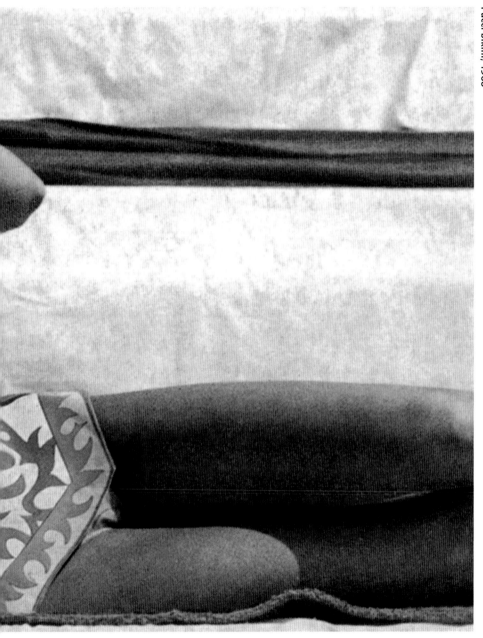

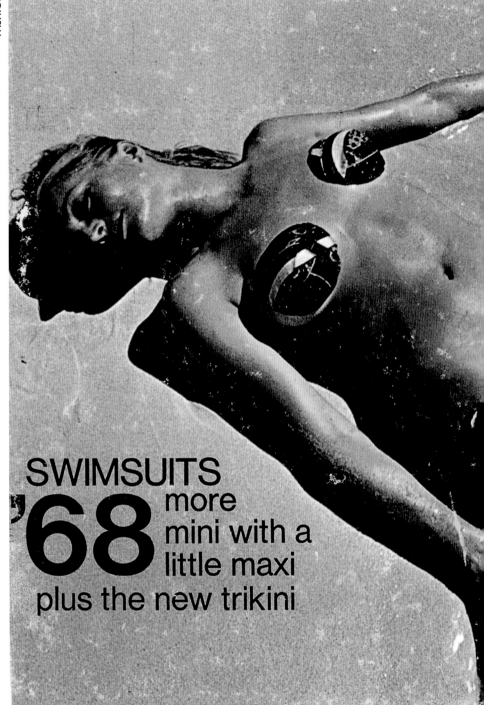

SWIMSUITS
'68
more
mini with a
little maxi
plus the new trikini

of the bikini bottom and at the closure of the bikini top, the string bikini offered a new adjustability, allowing the wearer to show as much or as little skin as she wished. Triangle tops and bottoms almost completely supplanted the bandeaus, bikini briefs, and boy-cut bottoms of the 1960s. In 1974, Diane von Furstenberg re-engineered the two triangles as a bandeau, gathered at the center with a string halter at the sides, lifting the breasts without linings or foundation.

Exposure was further welcomed in the '70s with an ERES bikini featuring a top that untied in the front to increase tanning. Meanwhile, Parisian designers had fully entered the scene with Dior for Saks Fifth Avenue bikinis, one of which was featured in photographer Deborah Turbeville's famous bathhouse spread in the May 1975 *Vogue.*

Also invented in the '70s was the thong, for which American designer Rudi Gernreich took full credit in 1974. Defined as a bikini bottom with a back so thin it disappeared between the buttocks, Gernreich's thong was featured in fashion magazines, but not as swimwear. Sometimes referred to as a tanga or G-string, the thong was used to dramatic effect by *Vogue* magazine darling Giorgio di Sant'Angelo, whose version appeared in the *Sports Illustrated* swimsuit issue in 1975. Though it originated in the '70s, the thong was not fully embraced until much later.

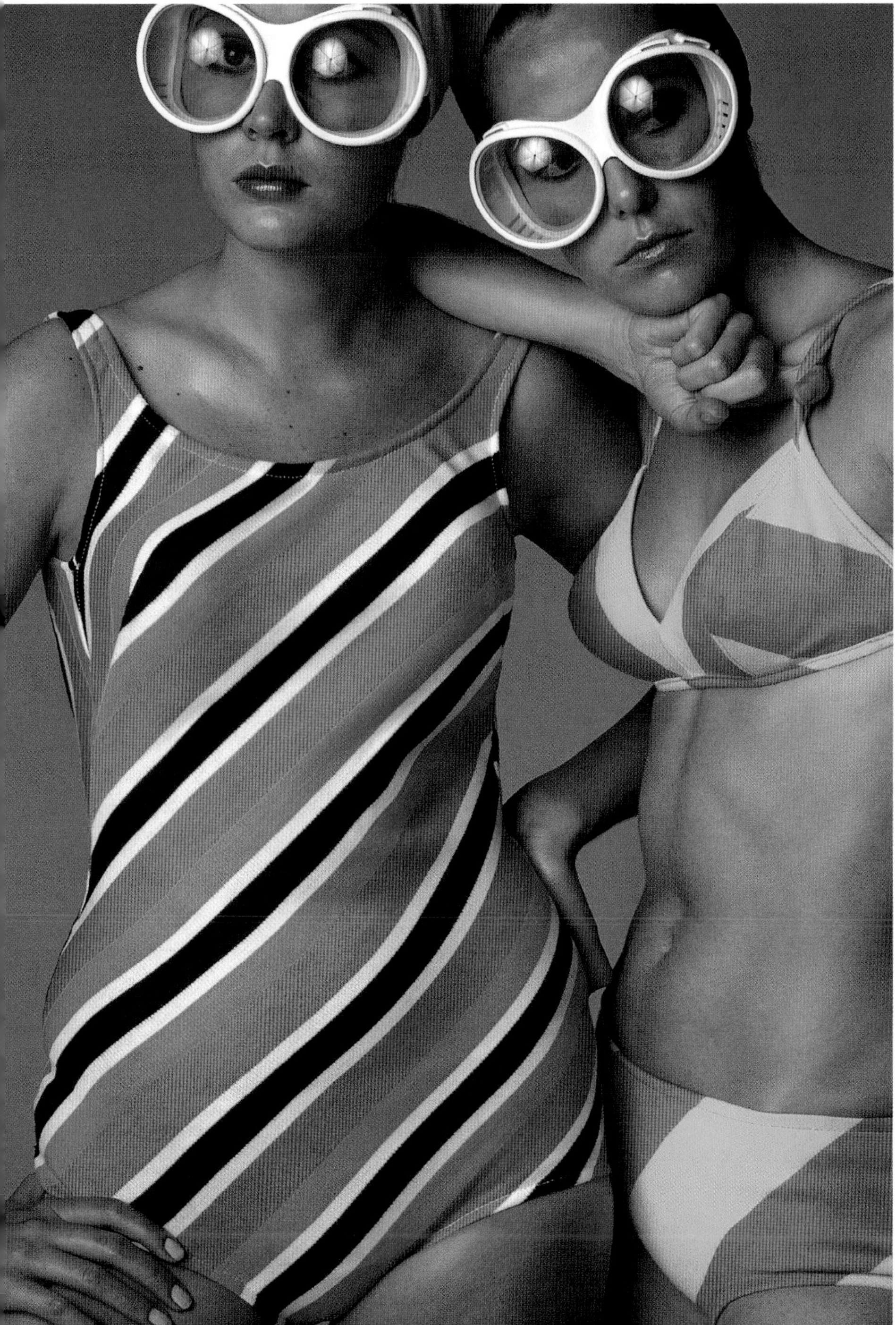

Cole of California swimwear, 1967

THE RIGHT BIKINI
IS LIKE A PICTURE FRAME
THAT HIGHLIGHTS ALL THE
EROGENOUS ZONES.

MICHAEL KORS

MYTHOLOGY

RUDI GERNREICH

INNOVATOR AND ACTIVIST

In 1964, fashion designer Rudi Gernreich ignited a national debate over topless bathing with his creation of the monokini. This topless maillot was a design now feasible with the advent of LYCRA® which was invented in 1959 and could stretch up to seven times its original length without breaking and subsequently recover its shape.

To popularize his suit, Gernreich hired William Claxton to photograph his model and muse, Peggy Moffitt, in the monokini. These images entered the national consciousness after 19-year-old model Toni Lee Shelley was arrested and charged with indecent exposure on a Chicago beach. Gernreich's creation then appeared in *Life* magazine on October 4, 1964 with an image of Moffitt with her hands folded over her breasts.

I NEVER DREAMED IT WOULD GO BEYOND THE FASHION BUSINESS INTO SOCIOLOGY.

RUDI GERNREICH

EIGHTIES AND NINETIES

The major innovation of the early '80s was the leg line of the bikini bottoms, which began to work its way up toward the natural waist, creating a V shape and giving the appearance of length to the legs. Roll-style bathing suits, which could be adjusted to expose as much or as little as wanted, were the bikinis of choice—that is, for women who still went into the sun, despite the new warnings about skin cancer.

Another trend in the '80s was Day-Glo, which was manifest on swimwear by Body Glove, a scuba and surfwear wet suit manufacturer, which constructed neon-colored suits made out of neoprene. Also in the late '80s, the J. Crew catalog created a sensation in America by selling tops and bottoms in different sizes and colors, while the fashion brands Dim and Huit popularized mix-and-match in France.

As recognized designers began to incorporate the bikini into their collections, luxury versions of the bikini began to appear. Suddenly, it became possible to sunbathe in Dior, Chanel, Versace, or Geoffrey Beene. During the '90s, French couturier Azzedine Alaïa took the gingham bikini popularized by Brigitte Bardot in the '50s out of St. Tropez and onto the streets of Paris with oversized gingham prints from the French store Tati. The "short and bra" ensemble became a huge sensation, bigger even than the playshort of the '50s.

In the U.S., Calvin Klein's minimalism served as a foil to Alaïa's and Norma Kamali's designs by using nude and muted-tone bikinis. Klein encouraged a new trend in swimwear that mirrored

underwear with minimal, subtle designs that accentuated the body in its entirety. Other designers also offered swimwear in their trademark styles. At Gucci, Tom Ford exploited sex with bikinis that were tight, black, and very sexy. Ralph Lauren took suede off the ranch and onto the string bikini. Lauren also embellished solid-colored bikinis with his Polo logo. And who could forget German designer Karl Lagerfeld's 1996 "eye-patch" bikini for Chanel. The top consisted of button-sized double-C logo disks with strings attached; the cost: $465.

The most remarkable aspect of '90s bikini design, however, was the triumph of the thong. This was shown to best advantage in a May 1992 *Vogue* fashion spread which featured an Isaac Mizrahi bikini that invoked Claire McCardell's classic "diaper" swimsuit of the '30s, but with a thong back. The brevity of the bikini continued with the "microkini," a term coined in 1995 to describe ever smaller forms.

The underwear as outerwear trend of the '90s found expression in swimwear with the return of underwires, and lace and eyelet details. The Victoria's Secret catalog featured swimwear with lingerie-like features such as push-up bra tops. On the other side of the spectrum, the athletic tankini, which used LYCRA®, rather than underwire and boning for support, was also introduced.

Nowadays, every woman of every age wants to—and does—wear a different kind of bikini: the mini bikini, V-kini, thong, tankini, bandeau, halter-style bikini, low-rider, or roll-down, in gold, in furs, feminine ruffles, tribal details, suede, leather, boho chic, color block, minimal, '40s-inspired, '60s hip-riders with baby doll cover-ups, plaid bikinis, boy-cut briefs, luxurious silk- ribbon-crocheted bikinis, shiny lamés—whatever the style, fabric, and details, the bikini has always mirrored fashion trends.

A BIKINI IS SEXY WHEN THE WOMAN WEARING IT IS VIEWED FROM THE BEACH AS SHE IS WALKING ALONG THE OCEAN'S EDGE.

RICHARD MEIER

A SUN-KISSED BIKINI BODY FLATTERS ANY OUTFIT THAT FOLLOWS.

BRETTE SANDLER

A BIKINI DEFINES A WOMAN'S CURVES AND ACCENTUATES WHAT GOD HAS GIVEN HER... THAT'S SEXY.

JENNIFER LOPEZ

NUDITY IS CONFRONTATIONAL AND THE BIKINI IS INVITING

NORMA KAMALI

SKIN AND A TAN
MAKE THE BIKINI SEXY.

ELLE MACPHERSON

Lucky white bandeau top and belted bottom, 2006

Q&A

Norma Kamali

The leader of swimwear trends in the '80s was Norma Kamali, who revived the glamour and sex appeal of the '50s pinup with retro designs like high-hipped bikinis draped in jersey. In her OMO collection, Kamali showed much briefer versions of animal-print, and fringed bikinis, as well as gold and silver spandex string bikinis.

KKB: What makes the bikini sexy?
NK: The almost, but not completely, naked look, which is even sexier than being nude—most of the time...

KKB: What's the difference between the bikini and the two-piece?
NK: The bikini is sexy; the two-piece is style and fashion.

KKB: Who should wear the bikini?
NK: The bikini looks best on a well-proportioned body...and the best abs.

KKB: Who shouldn't wear the bikini?
NK: Anyone with a tummy.

KKB: Who is your favorite bikini-clad icon?
NK: I don't really have one, but all of the obvious work for me—Ursula Andress, Raquel Welch... but no one is sexier in a bathing suit than Marilyn Monroe in a two-piece.

KKB: What does the bikini say about the wearer?
NK: She is fit and comfortable with her body.

KKB: What's the sexiest bikini?
NK: There are so many, really, but

a good one is a nude, tiny bikini because it is there, yet not there... but I love so many types. Classic ones are always good.

KKB: Who's the sexiest man in a bikini?
NK: A skinny boy, no older than 21.

KKB: What's the sexiest fabric for a bikini?
NK: There is no limit. It's really about the combination of fabric and design. I love second-skin fabrics, but with any fabric, I could do a bikini and really like that too.

KKB: What's sexier: lurex, snakeskin, or black?
NK: It depends on the wearer. A bikini only works in combination with the spirit of the woman in the suit, so all three are very sexy, but if the wearer isn't feeling it in the most natural way, it won't work.

KKB: If you could use any material for a bikini, what would it be?

NK: A new, high-tech fabric that dries quickly, feels like silk, and can wear for twenty-five years, at least. And if it is sexy at the same time, that is what makes a bikini modern.

KKB: Is it better to conceal or to reveal?
NK: A good bikini must do both. Everyone wants to both accentuate and emphasize parts. It's rare to be able to reveal all. Concealing does have its virtues, however, even on the most perfect body.

KKB: What doesn't make the bikini sexy?
NK: Someone posing all the time in one. For example, holding their stomach, or not being comfortable with their body and the suit.

KKB: What's sexier in a bikini: full breasts or no breasts?
NK: No breasts, topless. Full breasts are too much, especially since most of them are not real anymore. Somewhere in between works best in a bikini.

Opposite and previous page (right):
Norma Kamali bikinis in Los Cabos, Mexico, 1995.

CHAPTER 6

THE MALE BIKINI

It is said that the best way for swimmers to optimize their performance is to swim naked. And no other suit comes as close to skin as the Speedo.

With the designs of this Australian company, men's swimwear was revolutionized. After turning ninety percent of its production over to the war effort, in 1949 the company made looser-fitting, navel-hiding, bikini-style swimsuits for the Australian Olympic Games. In the '70s, the LYCRA® Speedo, popularized by Olympic swimmer Mark Spitz, made headlines as the lowest-cut men's swimsuit ever made. Europe quickly adopted the fashion, while a more conservative America took time thinking it was too indecent, even though the swimmer's body—broad shouldered and lean—was (and is) the envy of every man. In the '80s, the legs were cut even higher, reflecting the Brazilian influence of the tanga; the men's bikini also got briefer because competitive swimmers believed it would shave seconds off their times. Hence, the Speedo serves both form and function.

In the twenty-first century, the Speedo reflects the fashions of the time. If the jean can go low-rise, then so can the Speedo. Not only is the Speedo the fastest men's swimsuit, but it is also the sexiest. Just ask menswear designer Tom Ford, who in the late '90s took the Speedo-style suit, which emphasizes the proportions of the torso, off the swim team and onto the runway.

The male bikini is every inch as sexy as its female counterpart. Opposite, the bikini in Sydney, Australia, 2005.

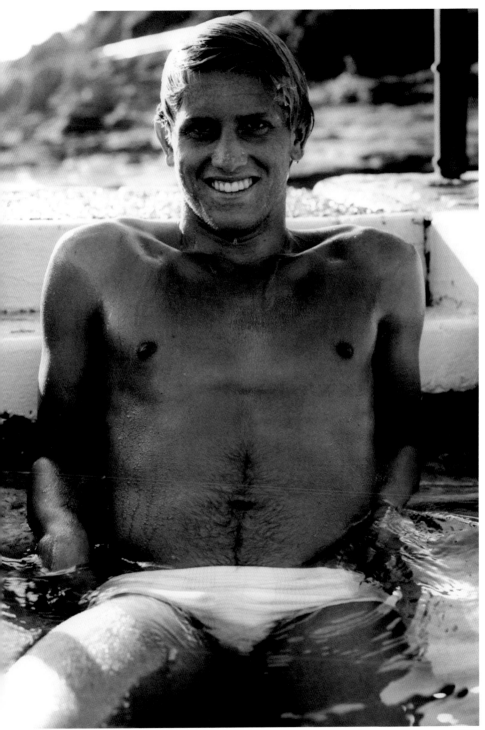

SPEEDO
IS TO BIKINI AS KLEENEX
IS TO TISSUE.

"THERE IS NO SUCH THING AS SPENDING TOO MUCH MONEY ON A BIKINI," MY MOTHER ONCE TOLD ME. "FRANKLY, IT'S MOST IMPORTANT TO LOOK YOUR BEST WHEN YOU ARE WEARING THE LEAST."

GIGI MORTIMER

TARZAN & JANE

It can be said that the origins of the bikini date back to primal man. In the twentieth century, obsession with the jungle came with D. W. Griffith's silent film *Man's Genesis* in 1912. *Tarzan and the Apes*, the first Tarzan film based on the writings of Edgar Rice Burroughs, followed in 1919. And in the '30s, swimmer and heartthrob Johnny Weissmuller further promoted the loin-cloth look.

Above: Bo Derek in *Tarzan the Ape Man*, (1981).
Opposite: Johnny Weissmuller as Tarzan in 1932.
Following pages: Maureen O'Sullivan in *Tarzan and His Mate* (1934) (left);
Caspar Van Dien in *Tarzan and the Lost City, (1998)* (right).

CHAPTER 7

THE BIKINI ON VACATION

With the advent of the birth control pill in the late '60s, sexual exploration soared. Exhibitionism was thought of as a way to show empowerment and independence. It was the jet age, and it was hard not to have a bikini. With every destination now accessible via airplane, you could roll up your bikini and be on the beaches in Florida, California, or even Europe in hours. From Malibu to Marbella, the bikini came to signify good times, high spirits, and a newfound energy.

Yet, in 1964, the Vatican banned the usage of the bikini in Catholic countries like Italy and Spain. In Belgium and Australia bikinis were boycotted as well. In conservative America, no woman of class would be seen in this scandalous suit, and if she was, she would be escorted off the beach. For many, the bikini conveyed liberation after World War II, while for others it conveyed too much.

אוטומטית
AUTOMATIC
SHOWER

THE SEXIEST THING ABOUT A BIKINI IS THAT IT LEAVES SOMETHING TO THE IMAGINATION, WHICH IS THE BEST PART.

ANNA SUI

SKIN IS SEXY.
BODY SHAPES ARE SEXY.
IT'S NOT THE BIKINI.
IF A WOMAN IS SEXY,
SHE IS SEXY, NO MATTER
WHAT SHE IS WEARING.

ANGELA MISSONI

269

WHAT MAKES A BIKINI SEXY IS THE BODY THAT WEARS IT... IT HAS TO BE AGILE AND HAPPY.

DIANE VON FURSTENBERG

ISLAND STYLE

PARADISE FOUND

Hawaii and the Polynesian islands have always been synonymous with one word: *paradise*. In the aftermath of World War II and the looming Cold War, Americans and Europeans alike were captivated by exotic and faraway places. A surf culture emerged, and traditional aloha and Hawaiian prints decorated everything from string bikinis to mini-sundresses. With its indigenous watermen, exotic women, and surfers, and plenty of unchartered territory, the islands in the Pacific were a dream.

A Polynesian woman drinks cocunut milk in Papeete, Tahiti (above) and the back view of an islander with flowers in her hair, (opposite).

281

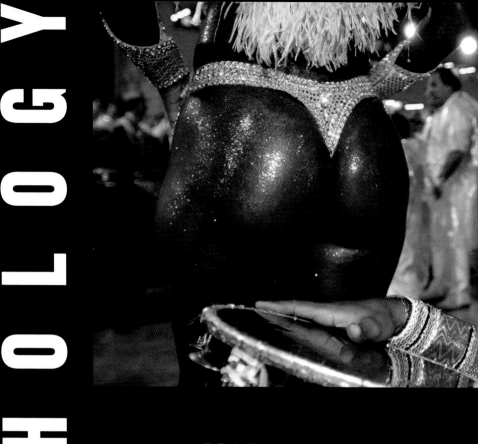

BRAZIL

HER NAME SHOULD HAVE BEEN RIO

Above and opposite:
The tanga style
on dancers in Rio
de Janeiro's Carnaval.

Following pages:
Rio de Janeiro
beach, 1984 (left);
a congressional
candidate puts his
campaign on his
daughter's bikini
on Ipanema Beach
(right).

In 1964, Antonio Carlos Jobim ignited the sound of bossa nova when he sang about "The Girl from Ipanema," an ode to local beauty. This song spurred the fantasy of Brazil and its alluring new bikini called the thong, tanga, or sunga (for men), inspired by Rudi Gernreich's 1964 design and by sumo wrestlers' suits— mini triangles held up by spaghetti strings. A few years later, the backless G-string bikini came out as a modified version of the

Above and left:
Helô Pinheiro,
"The Girl from Ipanema"

Following pages: A thong
(left), and matching bikinis
(right) in Buzios, Brazil.

original tanga, which accentuated full, voluptuous buttocks. *Newsweek* magazine called this new swimsuit phenomenon, *fio dental,* or dental floss. But Brazil wasn't always the liberated haven it appears to be. In Quadros, a right-wing conservative, wanted to sweep away corruption and prohibit bikinis on beaches of Rio de Janerio. In 1961, the mandate was lifted. Yet topless bathing is still prohibited in Rio today.

THE BIKINI IS THE PETER PAN OF FASHION. IT IS A RIGHT OF PASSAGE: AGELESS.

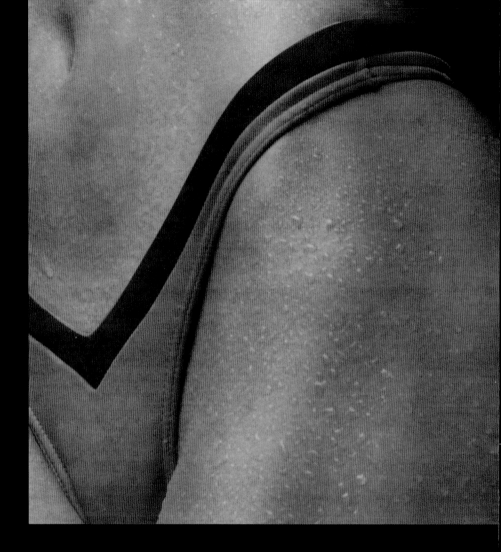

Above:
Bumbum thongs.

Previous page:
Girls on Copacabana beach.

Following pages:
Local women on a tourist
beach, Santa Maria del Mar,
Cuba.

CHAPTER 8
SURF, SPORTS, AND FUN

Surfing culture goes beyond simply knowing how to move across waves. A surfer's mind-set has to fuse with nature and space. It can be said that his or her philosophy best matches that of a '60s hippie. At the junction of sun and ocean, the surfer's body must be healthy and strong so that it can retain its youth as long as possible. In this incredibly picturesque world, set against the beaches of Hawaii, California, Australia, or Peru, pretty girls are part of the scene, and they cleverly compete with one another in their form of dress: the bikini.

Here, on a surfer's beach, one is likely to see the most flattering styles, since they're worn by sexy women, their bodies chiseled by the sport. Over the past ten years, surfing has grown increasingly popular with girls, who tend to practice it in bikinis. The photographer Bruce Weber has made quite a contribution to popularizing the sport, especially through his handsome advertising campaigns for Calvin Klein and Ralph Lauren.

Vivacious and spirited, the bikini has come to signify good times. Opposite, a football fan enjoys herself in Miami Beach.

303

SINCE THE BEGINNING, THE BIKINI HAS REPRESENTED FREEDOM, FUN, AND A SENSE OF LIBERATION.

MALIA MILLS

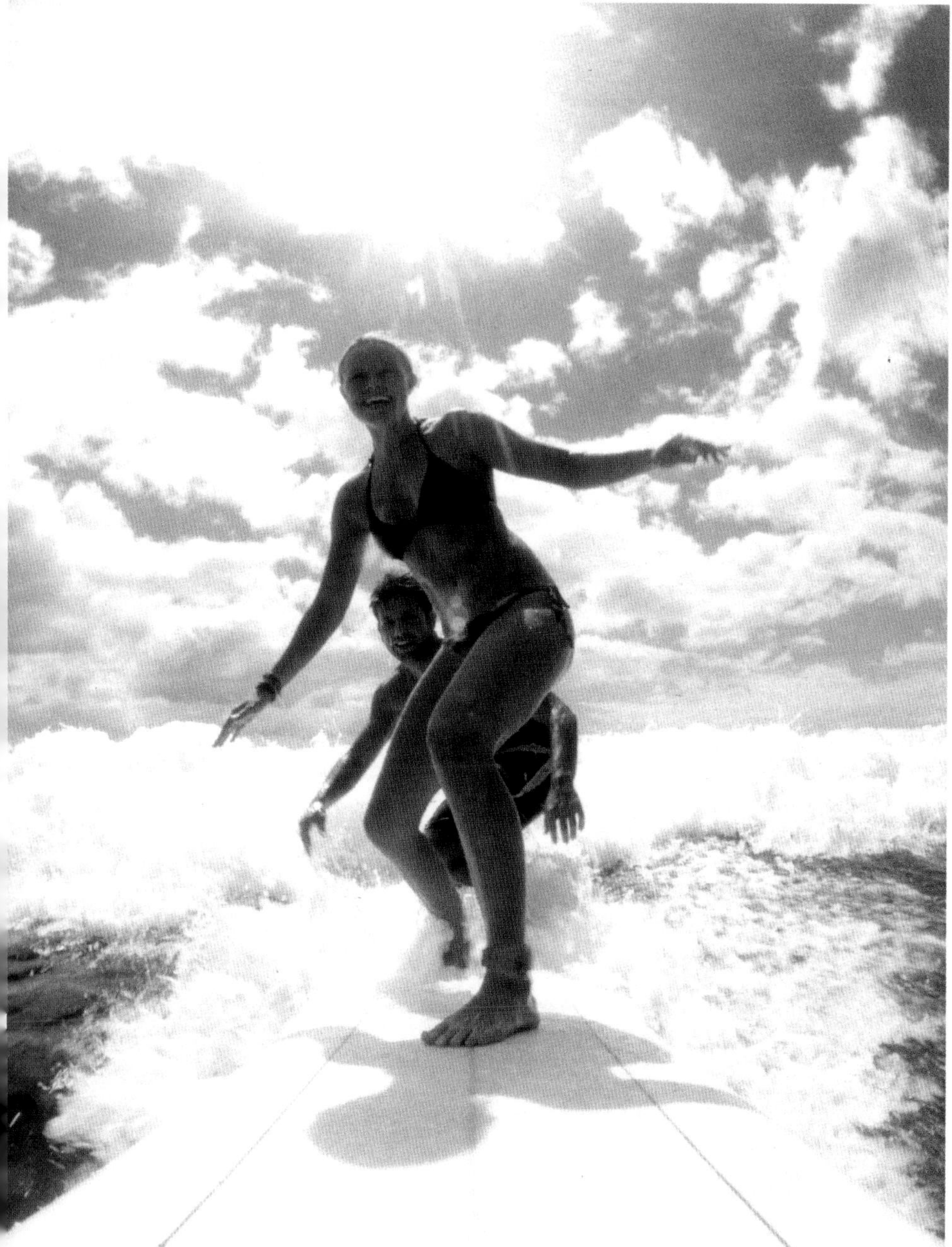

A scene from *Blue Crush*, 2002

MYTHOLOGY

BEACH VOLLEYBALL
THE UNIFORM OF CHAMPIONS

Pro Beach volleyball player/model Gabrielle Reece popularized the hugging halter top called the sports bikini. And in 1996, the bikini became the official uniform for the Olympic sport of beach volleyball. One of the only sports where athletes are instructed to wear a uniform that does not exceed a certain size, beach volleyball's mandatory dress code has received criticism as overly sexual and a ploy to increase viewers and gain sponsors.

Already a big draw for male and female viewers alike, American athletes Misty May-Treanor and Kerri Walsh further popularized this visually irresistable sport with a gold medal victory in August 2004.

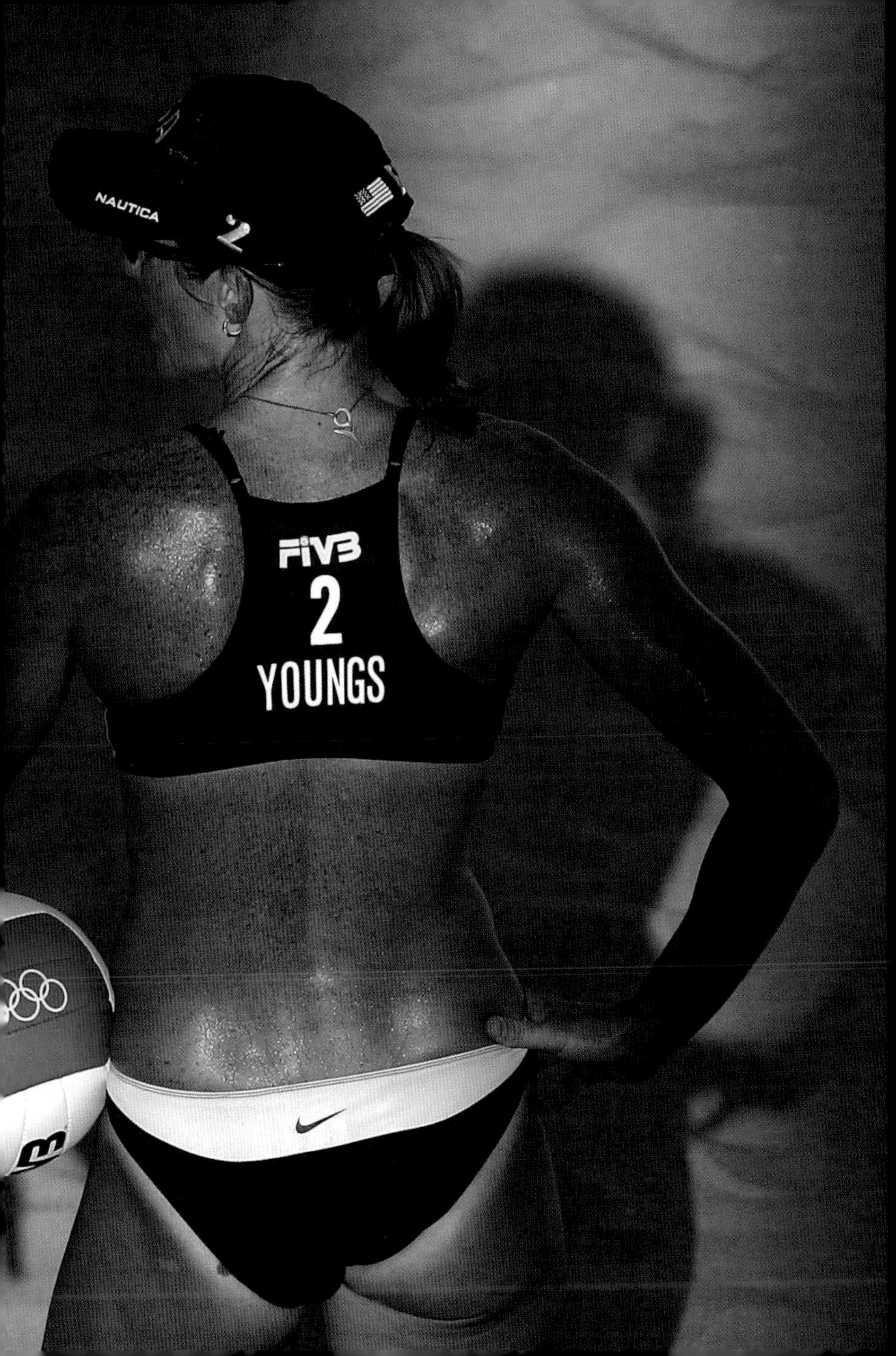
NAUTICA
FIVB
2
YOUNGS

Previous page:
Elaine Youngs at
the Athens 2004
Olympics.

This page:
Volleyball matches
in Manhattan Beach,
California (top), and
in Boulder, Colorado
(bottom) in 2005.

Opposite: Kerri
Walsh and Misty
May-Treanor in
Belmar, New Jersey,
2005.

Q & A

Gabrielle Reece

Mother, pro beach volleyball player, model, and wife clues us into her favorite bikini anecdotes, and how the bikini is both the most functional and most provocative uniform in the Olympics today.

KKB: What makes a bikini sexy?
GR: It is how comfortable the person seems to be who is wearing it. I learned from the Brazilian girls, who wear tiny bikinis and don't even think about it, that confidence makes a bikini sexy.

KKB: Who is the sexiest bikini-clad woman?
GR: Brazilian volleyball players and, of course, Gisele Bundchen. Hot chicks with boy hips and breasts don't hurt.

KKB: When did players start wearing bikinis for beach volleyball?
GR: Kathy Gregory and Nina Mattheis wore bikinis. The cut was more athletic because they didn't have the same high-performance material that has revolutionized the swimsuit industry.

KKB: Why did you wear a bikini for beach volleyball?
GR: The first year, I wore a sports bra and leggings. And then it became the uniform. It was actually

IT'S NOT THE BIKINI, IT'S THE WOMAN IN THE BIKINI.

TRACY FEITH

easier, because when you are hot and all the sand is everywhere it is easier to clean up, and you are obviously cooler. The bikini was much more functional.

KKB: What is the best style to play in?
GR: The best is the two-piece with enough coverage on the buttocks. As far as the top goes, there is a fine line. It can't have too much fabric, but we are already muscular and don't need to overaccentuate that, but it can't be too little, where you fall out while you are going for

a ball. And triangle tops that slide don't work.

KKB: Would Laird ever wear a bikini?
GR: I have asked him, and he says, "No way baby." But wouldn't it be great to see him riding a huge wave in a Speedo.
KKB: I want a photo of that.

KKB: Who is the sexiest man in a bikini?
GR: Well, I would say you-know-who, but he won't wear a bikini. It would have to be either a swimmer

or a diver. Greg Louganis when he
was competing.

**KKB: What's the best fabric for
a bikini?**
GR: You can't beat LYCRA®.
And, the combo of LYCRA® and
a polyester would be great—for it
would be more durable, hold its
structure, and keep its shape.

**KKB: What is the worst fabric for
a bikini?**
GR: Crochet. It gets wet and it's
all over.

**KKB: What's sexier, a boy short or
a bikini?**
GR: A brief is good for teens with
no hips. A woman should only wear
a bikini.

**KKB: If you could be anyone in
a bikini, who would you be?**

GR: It took me 35 years to be okay
with myself. I remember growing up
in the Virgin Islands as a teenager.
It was painful. Teenage years are
probably when you look the best,
but I felt miserable.

**KKB: What is your best memory
of the bikini?**
GR: One of my oldest memories
was when I was young, boogie-
boarding all day long in my bikini.
And my most recent best memory
is when I got married in a bikini
covered by a sheer dress. As soon as
we got married, I took off my dress
and went swimming.

**KKB: What does the bikini
represent for you?**
GR: It represents everything
I love: the beach, the water, and
the fresh air.

IT DOESN'T MATTER HOW THIN OR FAT YOU ARE OR HOW BIG YOUR BOOBS ARE, LOOKING SEXY IN A BIKINI IS JUST ABOUT HAVING THE RIGHT ATTITUDE. HOLD YOUR HEAD UP AND WALK PROUD!

SIMON DOONAN

Los Cabos, 2005

WHAT MAKES
A BIKINI SEXY IS THE MIND
PERCEIVING IT AND
THE BODY WEARING IT.

STEVEN KLEIN

CHAPTER 9
EXTREMELY BIKINI

The bikini is, of course, a tool for seduction. But it's also an extreme sport uniform. Certain designers, namely creative ones, haven't been able to resist transforming these strategically placed bits of fabric in ways that attract everyone's eye, including the camera's.

Austin Powers and the Fembots, those charming female robots with bikini tops-cum-smoking guns are perfect examples of how far the concept of the bikini can go. In reality, the Brazilian tanga, or thong—also called dental floss—could be pushing the envelope on decency, for it's hard to conceive of something smaller to follow.

Although it was first considered provocative, the Brazilian bikini has since become the norm. At this point, its form can be found in women's lingerie around the world, rendering classic underwear almost obsolete. And today teenagers take pleasure in having their thongs peep out of their low-cut jeans. Along with piercings and tattoos, the Brazilian tanga reflects an era, and

Opposites attract in the most outrageous swimming costumes. once again points to how bikini trends influence the style of women's intimate apparel.

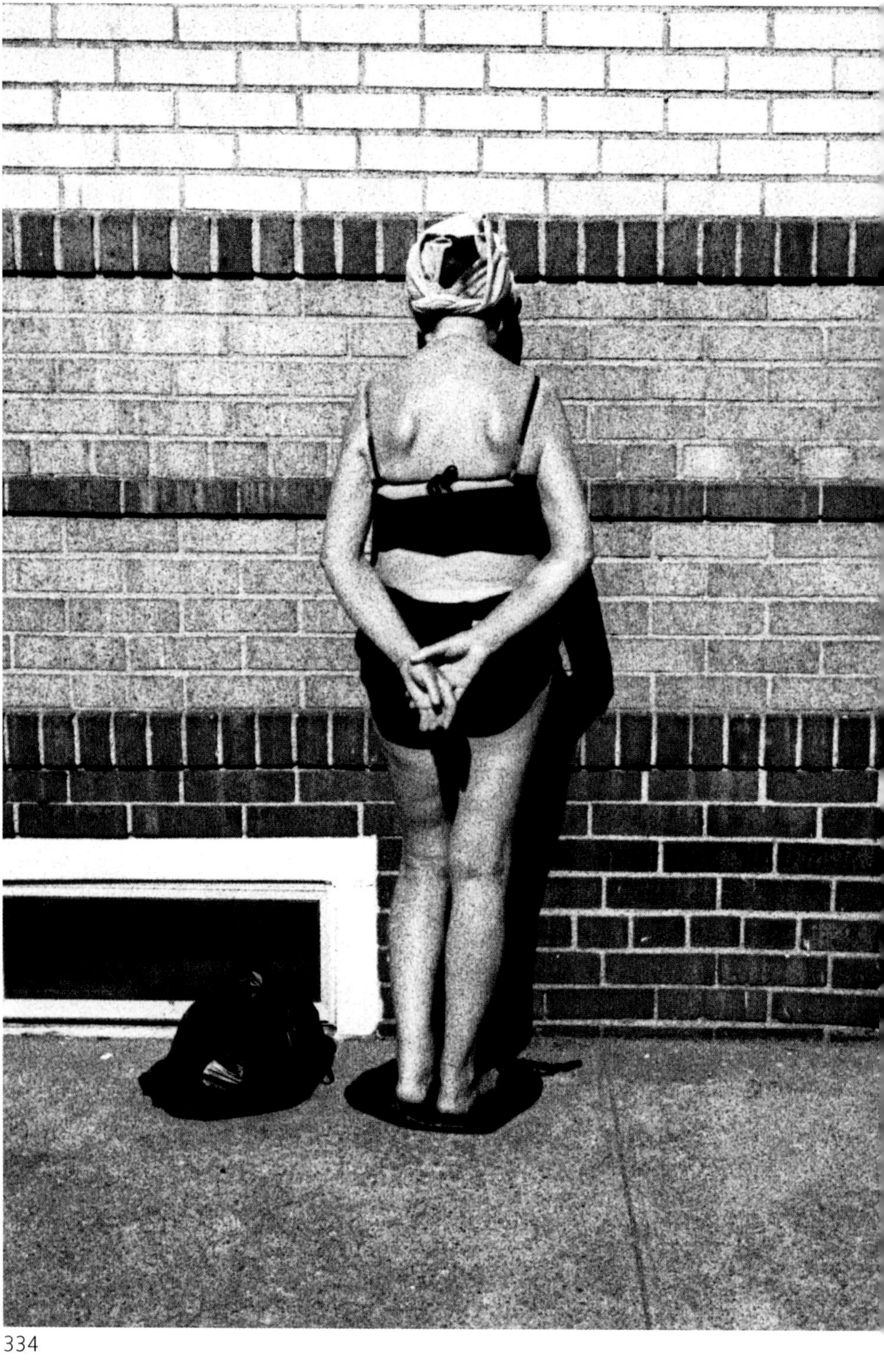
Bleecker Street, New York, 2000

The tanga on Copacabana Beach, Brazil

Union Jack swimwear in London's Trafalgar Square to promote tourism to Gibraltar

341

Left to right: 1. Tawny Kitaen (signed). 2. Madonna
(signed). 3. Brigitte Wilson (this one signed and
inscribed "To Richard Prince, off the best". 4. Helen
Christenson (signed). 5. Laetitia Casta (signed).

Untitled (Publicity) **by Richard Prince, 2005**

343

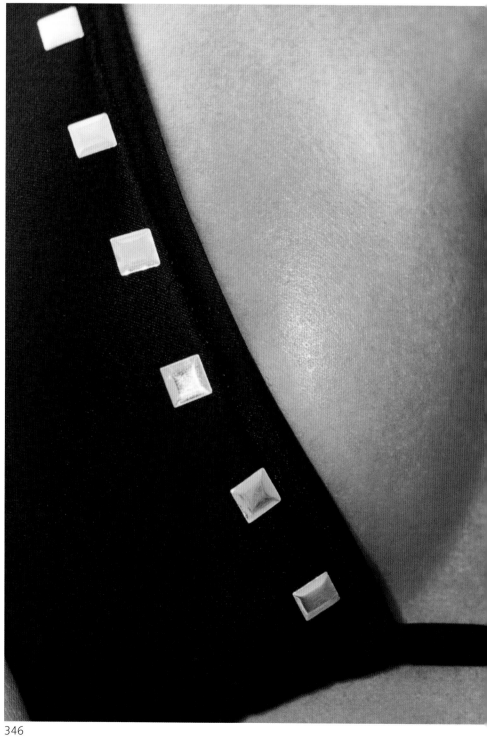

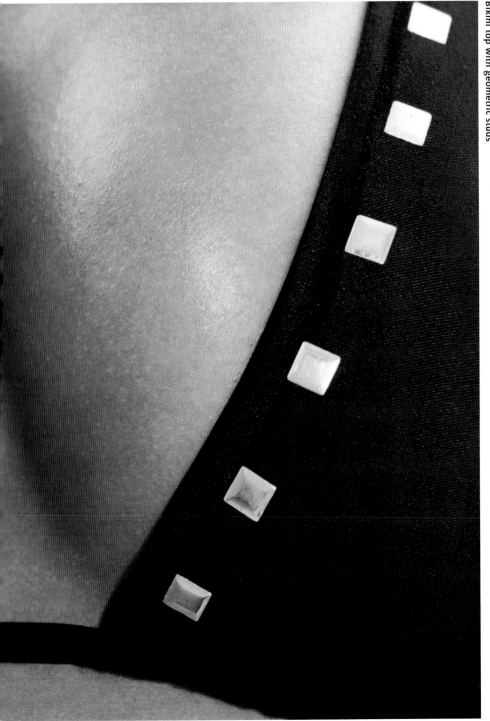

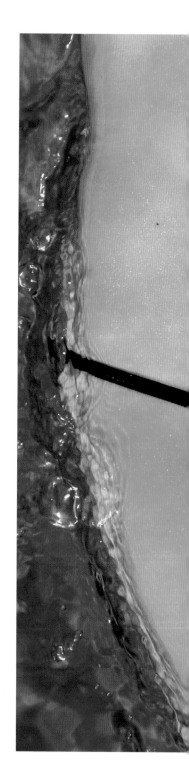

A BIKINI IS NOT A BIKINI UNLESS IT CAN BE PULLED THROUGH A WEDDING RING.

LOUIS REARD

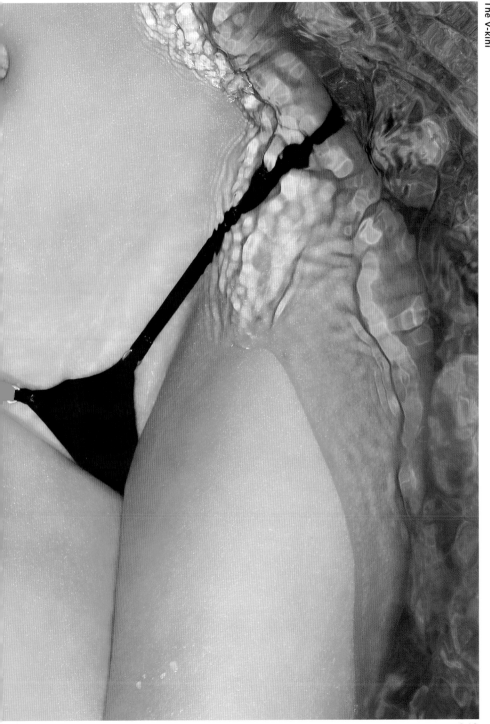

353

YOUR BODY IS A TEMPLE, BUT HOW LONG CAN YOU LIVE IN THE SAME HOUSE BEFORE YOU REDECORATE?

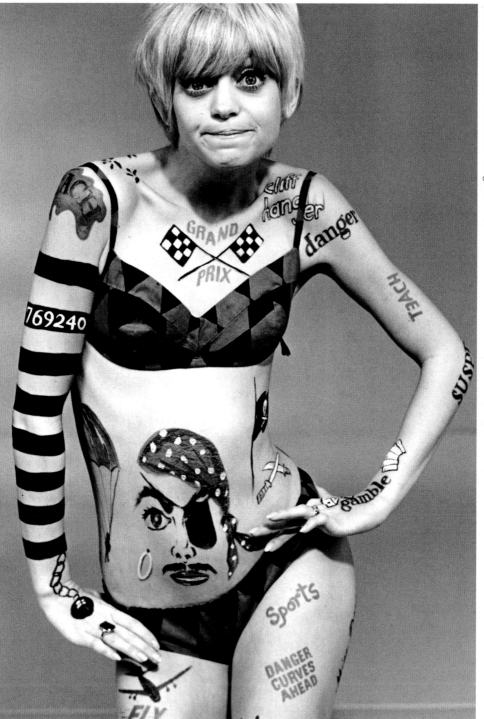

Girls prepare for a self-tanning session in Los Angeles

SPRING BREAK

THE BIKINI ON THE LOOSE

Ever since the first bikini, the choice of which style to buy has been difficult and crucial. A girl's body can change fast during her teenage years, as fast as a girl's taste, which is largely influenced by her friends and driven by advertising. Girls, many of whom have such complexes at that age, often choose their first bikinis with friends. They discover their own body shapes, they scrutinize their defects. They try to cover their weaknesses and bring out their assets. Personalities take shape. And seduction, even if it goes unacknowledged, is the primary reason for girls to travel to "bikini land."

Every woman remembers her first bikini. She "discovers" her body and has her first experience of being watched by members of the opposite sex. In the United States, a first bikini is often bought for spring break, a time of multiple indulgences, when new Lolitas show off their charms, often dangerously. These first sun-filled vacations usually include wet T-shirt contests, binge drinking, and all-night partying. Director Joe Francis perfectly captured this custom in his film *Girls Gone Wild,* which is filled with spring break fever.

Bossa n' St

The electro-bossa songbook of The F

FOOL TO CRY
LET'S SPEND THE NIGHT TOGETHER
OUT OF TIME
SYMPATHY FOR THE DEVIL
UNDER MY THUMB
SATISFACTION

HARLEM SHUFFLE
RUBY TUESDAY
ANGIE
MISS YOU
START ME UP / BROWN SUGAR
WILD HORSES

The Río SERIES

nes

g Stones

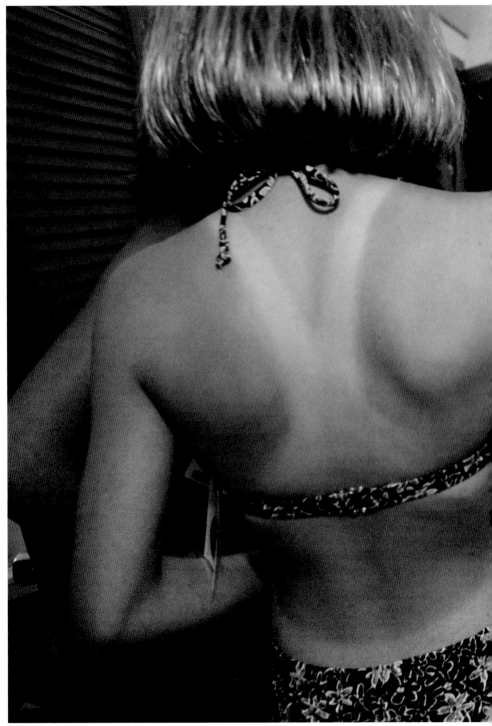

BIKINI CONTESTS

WET AND WILD

In September of 1946, California-born Marilyn Beuford was crowned Miss America while wearing a bikini. But in keeping with the country's conservative culture, the evening dress replaced the swimsuit in the following year and has been the deciding competition ever since. After 1951, the bikini was banned completely from the Miss World Contest, as the judges thought it gave some models an unfair advantage. Since the '50s, needless to say, pageants have changed their tune. In 2005, the bathing suit competition in the Miss America pageant is still one of its greatest attractions.

Though they are controversial, sexually biased, and above all, basal, bikini contests take place across the globe, from Cairo to Malaysia. Whether orchestrated by swimwear companies, the makers of suntan lotions, or rowdy bars and nightclubs, or even organized online, bikini contests foster a culture drenched with sexuality and pleasure.

I JUST USE MY MUSCLES AS A CONVERSATION PIECE, LIKE SOMEONE WALKING A CHEETAH DOWN 42ND STREET.

ARNOLD SCHWARZENEGGER

BODYBUILDING

THE FOUNDATION OF THE BIKINI

Bodybuilding is defined as "the use of progressive resistance exercise to control and develop one's musculature." Progressive resistance exercise is made possible by using barbells and dumbbells, or machine stations, at progressively heavier weights. When done consistently, bodybuilding can enhance a man's—or a woman's—appearance and sense of strength. The first famous bodybuilder in the late 1800s, Eugen Sandow, got his start as a professional strongman. In 1898, he even started publishing his own magazine, *Physical Culture*. Bodybuilding evolved with the times. In the '30s and '40s on Muscle Beach in Santa Monica, California, bodybuilders gathered to perform various stunts before the crowds. Among the usuals were Jack La Lanne, Joe Gold (founder of Gold's Gym), Harold Zinkin (inventor of the Universal Gym, the most widely used exercise machine), and John Grimek (Mr. America, 1946). With the beach comes the exploitation of the body. Surf sensation Laird Hamilton told his wife, volleyball player Gabrielle Reece, that "a body looks sexy when it looks like you can do something with it." In the '80s everyone wanted "to get physical," and the bodies reflected this desire. Men and women alike were obsessed with the way they looked in the newly popularized LYCRA®. All bodybuilding competitions were performed in bikini style suits for men and women. *Accentuate* and *enhance* are the operative words in bodybuilding, and the bikini manages to do both well.

Opposite:
Mr. Universe,
New York, 2000.

EVERY MAN IS
THE BUILDER OF A TEMPLE
CALLED HIS BODY.

HENRY DAVID THOREAU

4

COPYRIGHTS

ACKNOWLEDGMENTS

Special thanks to:

The Bikini Book would never have occurred without the genius idea from James La Force and Leslie Stevens and Hachette Publications.

To my parents who taught me to swim my own race and focus on the task at hand.

To Gilles Bensimon who has always supported me, and taught me that I can do a lot more than I think I can.

To my beautiful girls, who for me, put the "i" in bikini.

Thank you to Martine and Prosper Assouline, who encourage me to think out of the box, and push me into uncharted territory. I am so grateful for every opportunity you have ever given me.

To Harold Koda and the Costume Institute for opening up my mind and for nurturing my love of exploring high and low. "If it's good, it's good."

Thank you to my assistant, Lauren Cooper, who never gets overwhelmed, and always reminds me every day to "stay calm."

To Tomas Maier who has inspired me with his amazing bikinis and pool wear. Maier's swimwear designs supersede bathing suits; they are works of art that allow a woman to look like a woman.

To Dyonne Venable who never watches the clock, and who always makes you feel like you are the only person in the world, and whose help is without condition. Technically she does work for Gilles Bensimon.

To Jack Kliger, the president of Hachette, who has always seen me as my own person, and who has given me the opportunities to explore a world of magazines. He has made my dream a reality.

To Barbara Friedman who supports my far-fetched ideas, and sees them as plausible.

To Guillaume Bruneau who has taught me restraint and how not to exploit, and encouraged me to explore and fine-tune my obsession with high and low. An image tells a story; it catalogues a moment you can never repeat.

To my dear friends Andrew Bolton and David Vincent, who encourage me to do it my way. I am grateful for their friendship and for always believing in me, even though I make them crazy with my hundreds of questions.

To the entire ELLE staff who have always gone out of their way to facilitate all of my requests and have made this book such an easy process.

To Esther Kremer and Sebastien Ratto-Viviani who made sense of all of my text and photographs. A book is an organic process. I am grateful for their flexibility, steadfastness, and willingness to always keep an open mind. Rome wasn't built in a day, but this book was built in three months.

To Carol Smith who always encourages me to keep moving forward, and tells me that I can do it all.

To James Booty who came in at the final hour, his calmness coupled with his legal sense kept me on track and determined. Thank you, James.

Thank you so much to all of the photographers whom I admire and who continue to inspire me on a daily basis. Their vision of what is beautiful has encouraged me to see truly beautiful images as iconic, and to appreciate unconventional beauty.

Thank you to all of my contributors and friends for your unconditional support. Walter Iooss, Pamela Hanson, Steven Klein, Bruce Weber, Richard Prince, Gilles Bensimon, Matt Albiani, Greg Morris, Greg Kessler, Larry Gagosian, Gladstone Gallery, Everett Collection, Ron Harvey, Joan Moore, Photofest, Ron Mandelbaum, Shawn Buchanan, Claudine Ingeneri, Nicole Will, Norma Kamali, Gabrielle Reece, Andrew Preston, Jessica Glasscock, Bunny Yeager, Ron and Betty Galella, Ivan Bart, IMG models, Jennifer Lopez, Michael McGraw, PETA, Alvaro, Nan Bush, Nathaniel Kilcer, Betsy Johnson, Malcolm Carfrae, Jenna Lyons, Jessica and Jerry Seinfeld, Toni Howard, David Yarnell, Calvin Klein, Derek Lam, Ellen Barkin, Richard Stark, Donna Karan, Elle MacPherson, Diana Picasso, Brette Sandler, Zac Posen, Liza Bruce, Pamela Anderson, Anna Sui, Tracy Feith, Angela Missoni, Simon Doonan, Richard Meier, Gigi Mortimer, Michael Kors, Tyra Banks, Patrick McMullan, Pam Geiger, Patrick McMullan, Garrison Keillor, Richard Meier, Elizabeth Hurley, Diane Von Furstenberg, Alex Badia, Peter Knell, Martin Lavoie, and Hong Li.

The publisher wishes to thank:
Marcia Terrones, Julian Cohen, Karen Carpenter, Helô Pinheiro, Cécile Goddet-Dirles, and all the models who agreed to be featured.

Thanks also to: LYCRA®, Jeff Walker, Bill Ghitis, Jon Penrice, Ninabeth Sowell, Dianne Lober, Robert Kirkwood, Linda Kearns, Fabianne Pacini, Lorenza Bassetti, Ebru Pirinccioglu, Andrea Cintra, Patricia Lam, Steve Stewart, Darlington Fabrics, Eurojersey, Hafner, Jersey Lomellina, Texollini, Tricot Liesse, United Textiles, Lunada Bay, Swimwhere Anywhere, Warnaco, Alison Sherman, Catherine Gardere, Nicole Tolmie, Deborah Ayerst, Amanda Marsalis, Tricia Burlingham, Peggy Sirota, Thierry Demont, Thomas Lisanti, and Leslie Rummel.

First published in the United Kingdom in 2006 by
Thames & Hudson Ltd, 181A High Holborn, London WC1V 7QX
www.thamesandhudson.com

British Library Cataloguing-in-Publication Data
A catalogue record for this book is available from the British Library

ISBN-13:   9-780-500-51316-3

ISBN-10:   0-500-51316-3

Printed in China